THE SOUTHLANDS OF SIVA: SOME REMINISCENCES OF LIFE IN SOUTHERN INDIA.

THE SOUTHLANDS OF SIVA: SOME REMINISCENCES OF LIFE IN SOUTHERN INDIA.

BY

A. BUTTERWORTH

Published by

Gyan Publishing House
5, Ansari Road
Daryaganj, New Delhi-110002
Phone: 011-47034999, 9811692060
E-mail: books@gyanbooks.com

Distribution Network
gyanbooks.com
India, USA, Canada, UK, Australia, France

ISBN : 978-81-212-4051-2 (PB)
First Published, London, 1923

2nd Impression 2020

Printed at: Gyan Press, Delhi.

TO

MY WIFE

IN MEMORY OF MY HAPPIEST

INDIAN EXPERIENCE

NOTE

In the Indian words (except those which have passed into current speech) pronounce the unaccented "a" like the "u" in "but" and the unaccented "u" like the "oo" in "foot." It has not been thought necessary to distinguish between the various forms of consonants, although, in the Dravidian languages, the hard and soft "d" and "t" differ considerably in sound.

CONTENTS

CONTENTS

THE SOUTHLANDS OF SIVA

CHAPTER I

SOUTH CANARA

"THE entrances of the elder world were wide and sure and brought immortal fruit." The angel's words serve to call up before me South Canara as it was when I first landed at Mangalore, well back in the nineteenth century. Since then, the railway has appeared upon the scene and has destroyed I know not what fine fragrance of remoteness and flavour of antiquity. Fortunately, however, Canara's cup of enchantment contains ingredients which are permanent.

The Ghāts form the eastern barrier of the district. They are shrouded in dark forest, but out of it push smooth green summits, and great to the man in the heat below is the appeal of those high-hung lawns. The midlands consist of a low plateau of laterite, a stuff neither rock nor soil and of so warm a red that in certain lights it takes on the colour of blood. On that upland you will hardly find other crop than scanty grass or other tenant than the plovers crying their plaintive question : "Did he do it? Did he do it?" But rivers have cloven wide ways through it, and rain has bitten into it a thousand dells with shaggy walls dropping sharply to carpets of vivid paddy patterned with gardens of plantains and lithe areca-palms. Beyond this tract lie the low, sandy coast and coco-nut palms in myriads. It is a land of effulgent sunsets. Each cloudless day ends over the motionless sea in profuse outpouring of gold and fierce pulsations of blinding flame. So Canara ; for three-fourths of the year, glowing under the sun or touched to more mysterious beauty by luminous nights ; for the rest, a gray shadow behind the rushing rain.

Over this country I wandered for a matter of two or three years. Tents are not in use, for they perish in the monsoon, but there are plenty of bungalows for travellers. Sometimes I trudged it on foot in no great contentment, for the climate does not encourage exercise ; besides I generally felt ill and had not then been broken in to loneliness. Sometimes I was on my Pegu pony, a kind of horse which is now, I believe, extinct, much to the loss of the world. Canara contains no horses (for the matter of that it contains no sheep either), and the appearance of an equestrian provoked great interest among the cattle. As I rode along, while the humbler sort of folk moved off the road before me in accordance with their respectful custom, there was a reverse movement on the part of the cows. With tails erect these came tearing in from all quarters and galloped alongside me until their curiosity was satisfied. Nor were other animals indifferent to my progress. On an occasion I came upon elephants hauling timber in the jungle, and one of them, catching sight of me, fell down straightway in a fit. There were no grounds for the suggestion that this occurrence was due to my style of equitation, for elephants have, notoriously, a dislike for horses and dogs. My Collector's fox-terrier routed a tusker out of the forest, and the welkin rang with the trumpeting of the creature as it fled in terror, with the dog yapping joyously round its heels.

I shall not attempt to delineate many of the

members of our little European settlement. A few, however, I may refer to, and I may say of all that in those unawakened days we dwelt on terms of amity with the natives of the country.

Moore was our District Medical Officer and I mention him first because of his eminence as a shikāri. His success was in proportion to his pertinacity. He would follow a herd of bison all day through the steaming jungle and, when night fell, cast himself down, with or without a trifle of food, to await dawn and the resumption of pursuit. His æsthetic qualities were evidenced by his burning down the summer-house which Basel missionaries with gross impropriety had planted on the majestic brow of the Kudiremukh.

Of his various hairbreadth escapes one must suffice. He had been reading about the correct way of picking up snakes and, seeing a snake on the floor, sought to put theory into practice with the result that he was bitten in the hand. Then he noticed that he had got hold of a venomous sort. By ruthless lancing and the use of nitric acid he averted death, but he lost the use of two fingers.

I had under me at one time a European sergeant who was adept at catching cobras. According to this authority, if you take hold of the tail and press it to the ground while pinching hard, the snake cannot reach back far enough to injure, and you can then dislocate its vertebræ by suddenly swinging it up and backwards. Or you can lay a stick on the neck and gently press the head to the ground, when the reptile will lie still; then you catch hold of the neck, just behind the head, quickly and firmly between thumb and forefinger. After this latter process the sergeant used to stitch the lips together with a needle and cotton. But most people content themselves with a less artistic application of the stick.

Recruitment for the Madras Army was so regulated that at one time the European officers of our regiment consisted of three colonels and a subaltern. These senior officers were severally distinguished for piety of a type rare in the tolerant atmosphere of an Indian station, for the ownership of a harem and for the possession of a taste, unique among Europeans, for the jack-fruit, the smell whereof is as that which drave Asmodeus into the utmost parts of Egypt. Naturally I was most intimate with the first, Colonel Macey to wit, and one or two little anecdotes occur to me as emanating from him. I never heard elsewhere of a venomous snake causing injury to man except by means of its fangs, but evidently that is possible, for Colonel Macey told me that on one occasion he was helping to dig a cobra out of a hole in a wall when the reptile suddenly popped its head out and spat over a space of a foot or two into the eye of one P. The regimental surgeon, Whiteley, gave me, however, the more probable version that the snake struck at P.'s face and, missing it, accidentally jerked some venom into his eye. Anyhow, P. was very seriously ill afterwards, his eye being so violently inflamed that his life was endangered, but in the end life and sight were saved.

Macey once upon a time, when marching with his regiment, went at the close of a stage to spend the day at a Travellers' Bungalow to which was attached a garden, perhaps one of those native gardens which I myself take a pleasure in, wildernesses of crowded trees and bushes pervaded with the steamy smell of water and the menace of lurking reptiles. At the house he was told that there was a tiger in the compound, and strolled out to see what had given rise to the fancy. As he was following a path among the shrubs, he saw a tiger turn into it. He dropped down into the undergrowth and awaited events. The animal lounged down the path, switching its tail, passed Macey within hand's reach, leapt over the wall and disappeared. I am not sure whether it was on the same march that the following incident occurred. As the regiment tramped along, the sound of a bell was heard in front, and the jingle grew until the cause was apparent, for they met, striding along, an ascetic who had not only discarded every vestige of clothing but, to emphasize his nakedness, had attached a bell to a portion of his person.

Another member of Mangalore military society was Woodcock, with whom I went once after some panthers which had taken up their abode in a small cave in one of those many adkas, or valleys, which score the laterite plateau. We had a goat tied up in front of the den and lay close by on the ground. In a clump of bushes by my side a panther lay for a time watching, its breathing plainly to be heard. Now and again a vague shape flitted past or over the goat which made piteous noises. But it was too dark to shoot, and so the hours went by until the tuk-tuk-tuk-tuk-trrr of the nightjar announced the pale, infiltering dawn. A day or two afterwards the goat died, as a consequence apparently of the fright it had undergone. Woodcock who was a little distance from me stated that, while watching, he fell asleep on his face and woke to find a panther standing with its forepaws on his shoulders. He had been at Port Blair, and I remember his telling in the mess a story of his harpooning a gigantic sunfish off the Andamans. After some moments of frenzy, the unfortunate fish set off at prodigious speed and, before it succumbed, had towed Woodcock's boat twice round an islet of considerable size. At the close of this narrative there was silence for a few minutes, and then the Colonel in a tone of quiet interest asked, "Did it perspire much?"

I may bring the jovial Sundius on the stage for an instant in order to attach to him two small snake-stories. He was standing on the beach when something hurtled through the air to his feet and at once sat up as a cobra. His first act was to remove himself, his second to scan the sky, where the presence of a kite explained the snake, though I have not come across any other instance of a kite carrying off a live snake. On another occasion he, with a peon, disturbed a cobra which unhesitatingly attacked them, a case unique in my experience. The pair fled with the snake in pursuit and, as they ran, the peon's turban fell off. The snake pounced on this, shook it as a terrier might a rat, and then retreated.

As June drew nigh we all, civilians and military, gathered together in Mangalore to undergo our annual season of mourning and bear up as best we could against the depressing influences of gloom, incredible saturation, and the unceasing clamour of wind and sea and of rain which in business hours roared like a cataract and at off times fell in drops "varying in size" (I quote from an Irish newspaper) "from a shilling to eighteenpence." When the monsoon is drawing to a close a ceremony is performed to appease the sea-deity. This occurs in August, and no boat may be launched beforehand. A principal feature is the throwing of coco-nuts into the sea, and generally some of the Europeans took a part in the proceedings. On the occasion when I did so the lucky time was fixed for 5.30 p.m. but, as some of us wanted to get away earlier, it was easily arranged that 4.30 should be reckoned as 5.30.

Another ceremony at which I remember to have been present was the Jubilee of Queen Victoria. This was celebrated by sports, of course, but also by attendance on the part of many of the Europeans at the religious services held at the various temples in Mangalore. Moreover, a meal was provided for several thousand beggars. One group of these unfortunates clouds my memory. Rodent diseases are rife on the West Coast. In mercy to others the victims usually go about with their deformities covered, but on this occasion they had bared their heads; not their faces, for they had none. Dreadful holes took the place of features. They were hardly human beings, rather spectres from some place of unutterable woe.

By mid-September one could generally venture out with safety into the green loveliness of the countryside. Not always so, however. One of the worst bits of rainy weather I have experienced was in that month, out Sirādi way. I had gone out there with Moore in the hope of catching some of those great carp which are commonly known as Mahseer and, also, of getting some shooting. On the first day we started off into the forest, picked up the tracks of a herd of bison and made after it. We caught up a tiger on the same errand as ourselves, but he refused to show himself and slunk off in the high grass, so we went on our way. Then the heavens opened and a sheet of water came down and continued to come down. I well remember our long return journey by way of the rocky stream-bed which formed the most convenient path through the jungle. The boulders were very slippery and Moore's tendency to trip and stumble had full play. Cries of rage and pain as he floundered into pools and came down on sharp points, falling on my ear from time to time, lightened my own labour. The following two days we were weather-bound and, seeing no probable end to the cataclysm, we abandoned the expedition. In those three days between twenty and thirty inches of rain fell. We got hold of a panther cub on this trip and Moore tried to feed it with milk through a catheter, but the ungrateful little beast only spat and scratched savagely. Finally, somehow or other, it escaped. I suffered another loss in the case of a Scaly ant-eater which had been found, washed pink by constant immersion, on the trunk of a floating tree. I gave it temporary quarters in my bathroom which had a solid brick flooring and deemed it safe for the night. But it dug up the floor and disappeared into the bowels of the earth.

The main quarry of the shikāris of the district was the bison, a noble creature which in Canara used to be deemed harmless. It is not, however, always so. I shall have occasion to mention later an adventure of Lascelles with one, and I have heard of other cases which expose the bison to the severe denunciation of the poet :

> " Cet animal est très méchant ;
> Quand on l'attaque, il se défend
> Avec férocité."

There was a planter on the Biligarangan Hills who was laid up for a long time as a result of being gored in the chest. A man I knew at Trichinopoly was charged by a cow-bison with a calf at heel and was very severely injured in the lower part of the abdomen. My friend Hatfield, again, when out with a companion, wounded a bull which charged the latter and a lively chase followed. Hatfield got in two more bullets and dropped the beast, but it staggered up, resumed pursuit, caught up the fugitive and, striking him with its forehead, flung him several yards. He was not, however, badly hurt.

Tigers were in places abundant and there was

one man-eater in the district. It frequented the coast-road and preyed in particular upon the postal-runners, who carry a spear bearing loose iron rings. The brute seems to have learnt to associate a clattering noise with the approach of a solitary man and laid its plans accordingly. One can imagine these tragedies. Darkness upon the deserted road, a distant jingle, and then the soft padding of running feet, yellow eyes aflame in a black clump of bushes, a cry, a brief scuffle, a pool of blood soaking into the dust. It was probably this animal which, north of Kundāpur, came on to the seashore one afternoon, in full daylight, and carried off one out of a party of Brahmans. This tiger was reputed to be a great traveller, covering fifty or sixty miles of a night.

Just about this time a Civilian in another district wounded a tiger and, although short-sighted and strongly warned of the risk, insisted upon wriggling after it into a thick patch of undergrowth. A native shikāri crawled in with him and, catching sight of the animal, made vain attempts to draw his companion's attention to it. As the latter was peering about, the tiger made its rush and drove its fangs through the young man's skull.

There was a diverting story about the effort of Spankie, another Civilian, to bag a tiger in South Canara, but, as I cannot tell it, I must content myself with two little anecdotes from another Province. One relates that a man and his wife went tiger-shooting on an elephant. A tigress was put up and wounded and made for the elephant. The elephant dropped on its knees to receive the attack, with the result that the riders were flung on top of the tigress which wriggled itself free and fled in terror. The other tale ends less happily. M., from an elephant, broke the back of a tiger. Its roars scared the elephant, which bolted towards the wounded animal. M., afraid of being swept off among the trees, clutched at a branch, and found to his dismay that he was hanging right above the tiger and also that his breeches were too tight to allow of his swinging himself on to the bough. In due time he dropped upon the tiger, which chewed his foot until a shikāri came up and killed it. M. lost his leg as a consequence.

I had for a few months charge of a portion of the Laccadive Islands and have ever since regretted that I did not take the opportunity to learn something of life on a coral island. The islands are divided between South Canara and Malabar, and I have a few stories to tell about them at second hand.

I think it was to Minicoy that my friend Hopley was sent to reinstate a Headman who had been expelled by his subjects. Hopley and the Headman left Malabar in a steamer which anchored some distance from the island. When the two men reached the shore in a boat, they found the islanders drawn up in a hostile mood, and Hopley made a speech inculcating submission to the Headman and the Power behind him. The gist of the response was that the Headman's decapitation was in the public interests and that, as Hopley had chosen to associate himself with him, he must expect the same doom. Hopley contested these illiberal views, and an argument ensued, the while one party advanced and the other retreated. When Hopley and the Headman had got knee-deep in the sea they surrendered, and they were conducted to the central jail of the island, which consisted of a hut harbouring mosquitoes of such size and ferocity that present torment almost extinguished fear of the future. When night fell, the prisoners set to work earnestly to effect an escape. Succeeding in this, they got to the shore, found a canoe and pushed off. Then lights sprang up behind them betokening discovery of their flight, and boats put out in pursuit, but after an exciting race, the fugitives reached the steamer with a few lengths to spare.

Two members of the Civil Service, Moroni and Powell, in the course of duty had occasion to visit one of the Laccadive Islands, and having landed them, the captain of their vessel went off for a fresh supply of coal. The Civilians found that the inhabitants of the island were suffering from scarcity of food but at first they were not seriously concerned for themselves ; they had provisions for six days and, though the fresh water available smelt atrociously, there was plenty of coco-nut water to take its place. As the days went by, however, M. and P. became rather anxious and laid a taboo on the solitary breadfruit-tree of the place with a view to their own sustenance. They fished diligently and they procured a small supply of rice, but, when the appointed period of six days had drawn out to treble that length without bringing the ship, vigorous measures became imperative. They secured a sailing-boat and a boatman, stowed a small canoe on board, and made for an island which was visible on the horizon in the hope of staying their appetites there. Halfway over there fell a dead calm and, resources on board being straitened, Powell took the canoe and started to paddle towards the place of refuge. He reached it, half dead, at nightfall and was greeted by a crowd clamouring for food. There was clearly nothing to be got there, and with a groan Powell threw himself on the sand and sought sleep. Later on the sailing-boat arrived. A day or so of misery followed and then smoke on the horizon revived hope. They embarked, hoisted the sail, and sped merrily along.

Then Powell fell overboard. For a space which seemed an eternity owing to the persistent tendency of his thoughts to the subject of sharks, he swam about, while the boat, under the guidance of Moroni, swept round him on strange and devious courses. At length Powell was hoisted on board and the voyage was resumed. Soon the steamer was neared and recognized as their own by two dirty and emaciated wretches wearing stubbly beards and most inadequate costumes. Fate had been unkind to them so long that it seemed to them natural to find themselves, when they gained the deck, under the curious observation of some neatly apparelled ladies who had been embarked at Calicut for a little cruise.

In the Canarese part of the islands there was in my time a plague of rats which did a lot of damage to the coco-nuts and, in response to complaints, a lot of cats were sent over. Then came laments that the cats were neglecting the rats and had themselves taken to climbing the trees and eating the nuts. For this unaccountable vagary no remedy suggested itself but, to cope with the continuing rat-nuisance, the Collector busied himself in sending over large owls, with what results I do not know.

Up to this time the inhabitants of the Amīndivis (so we call the Canarese group) had relied upon Faith-cures in their ailments, but the Government now decided to start there a dispensary under a Hospital Assistant. The islanders highly resented the innovation ; nevertheless, just before the monsoon broke, a very reluctant Hospital Assistant was shipped off in an open sailing-boat. The subsequent events were recounted in an entertaining report sent by the Hospital Assistant from somewhere in Ceylon to the Collector. It seems that the boatmen, infected by the island-spirit, made the man of medicine by no means a welcome guest on board. A high wind arose and the unhappy leech lay groaning in the bottom of the boat, where he was indifferently trodden upon by the crew. The boatmen also decided that, in view of the threatening aspect of the weather, it would be well to husband their resources, and, with this prudent object, they settled that their passenger should have no share in the food or water. They failed to make the islands, and the Hospital Assistant was ultimately landed in Ceylon in the last stages of inanition.

Close to the coast of Canara lie St. Mary's Isles. I pitched my tents in a clump of coco-nut palms on the quarter-mile of white sand and basaltic columns which constitutes Tonsepāru. I had as companion a man who, later, fell on evil days. We swam with some trepidation in the clear water and we shot blue pigeons. I am sorry to say that I shot my companion also, but he was not seriously injured. Further, with Boggu, our fisherman, we visited in a dug-out the cliff-bound island of Kappāy and the ruined fort on Bādagadda. The name Boggu means, by the way, charcoal, and is one of those depreciatory appellations which are given to appease the gods when these have given evidence of malevolence by causing the death of elder children in the family. Not far off, on the mainland, stands Udipi, where there is a *math* of great renown. This was presided over by an aged priest, who was, I believe, the thirty-fifth High Pontiff of all the Mādhvas and who was much venerated in the neighbourhood for a rare chastity. At his request I attended the ceremony whereat he nominated his successor. The transfer of sacred office to a little boy by the dying man whose countenance fully justified the reverence felt for him was a somewhat affecting scene.

The remoteness of the district has led to the preservation there in vigorous life of the primitive religion of

"Devil" worship, and I saw a "Devil" dance at Yēnūr. Several persons had been got up to represent these godlings, one of the performers being a quite ludicrously ugly old woman. The Fire-demon was distinguished by a brazier of fire on his head. Another person, figuring, if I mistake not, Kodumamuttayya, had a whitened face, an extraordinary garb composed of leaves, huge painted wings, and a sword, shield, and flyflap. All the performers hopped about and simulated possession, but Kodumamuttayya excelled in his howling and convulsive tremblings. I do not think that even his possession went very deep, for the tender of a rupee produced immediately a prophecy in Tulu that I should have abundant crops of coco-nuts and numerous children. The former part of this prediction has lagged in fulfilment.

At the same place I saw enacted with much verve a sort of religious farce. The actors wore masks supplied from a temple and some of these were delightfully comic. The costumes generally were most effective, and the troop of monkeys led by Hanumān was cleverly got up. When I left after some hours the progress of the play was interrupted by old Hanumān leaping off the stage and pursuing me down the road for a present.

That remarkable double peak known as The Ass' Ears is a favourite haunt of devils, but they also cling to high trees, whence they may drop on you if you venture underneath. They are so ubiquitous and mischievous that, as the Cherumars know, all deaths in Malabar are due to their agency.

The devils sometimes come into domestic relations with the people. In company with a native Roman Catholic official I was talking to a ryot one day on the subject of these beings and rather tactlessly asked him whether he believed in their existence. Adapting his remarks to his audience, he replied in the negative. Then a sense of his madness came upon him. He added hastily that he believed in one devil. This demon, he explained, inhabited the thatch of his own house, but it was a quiet, unobtrusive guest and made its presence known only by an occasional rustling or, when out of humour, by visiting the human members of the family with headaches. That conversation, as I remember, took place at Bantwāl, where the big river-fish roll up out of the depths to eat the rice thrown to them from the temple-steps. There was a dispensary there, and the then Hospital Assistant soon afterwards poisoned himself on reading the remarks which Moore placed on record as a result of his inspection of the institution. But the unfortunate man was perhaps more influenced by his recent discovery of signs of leprosy on his person.

Jainism is another religion which, practically extinct elsewhere in the Presidency, has lingered on in Canara. Even there the sect is small and dwindling, as a result, according to enemies, of the excessive amorousness of its members. The Jain temples are planned differently from those of the East Coast, being without the walls and great porticoes or gopurams characteristic of the latter; they have also sloping roofs and wooden superstructures with reversed eaves. The main portion of the building is of stone, and the carving thereon is often remarkable for beauty and finish. A conspicuous feature is the Kambha or Sthambha in front. This is a tall, slender stone column springing from an elaborate base and carrying a sort of pavilion or representation of a shrine. The excessive size of the capital, if one can call it by that name, gives a look of top-heaviness, but this is redeemed by the skill and taste with which it is adorned. Another peculiar lithic production of

Jainism is the gigantic statues of Gumatarāya, of which there are two in South Canara. They are not at all on a high artistic plane, but their size gives them impressiveness. The figures are naked, with representations of plants growing round the legs of the meditating devotee. That at Yēnūr is about 35 feet high and wears on its thick lips a smile in which I came to find a subtle wickedness which was almost attractive. The statue at Kārkal, on the shore of a delightful lake, is, if anything, taller, and near it is a pleasing temple called Chatramukh. Other noteworthy Jain temples are the fifteenth-century "bastis" at Mudubidre, one of which bears unaccountably the figure of a giraffe, and in the Priests' Cemetery at that place are to be found tombs the nearest analogues of which are said to be in Nipāl.

While on the subject of religions, I must not omit to mention the Roman Catholics, who supplied a good proportion of our officials in Canara. That body is sharply divided into those of Brahman descent and the rest. The former group are an intelligent and agreeable set of people, and both sets of people date back to Portuguese times. Their churches are quite a feature of the landscape, and the sight of them used to recall Europe to me in a comforting manner when I chanced to be feeling homesick. One such edifice, but that was in Malabar, was constructed, so they say, out of money secured by a lucky draw in the Calcutta Derby Sweepstake. It was not the original intention of the body of small Roman Catholic contributors who obtained the winning number to spend their gains in this way, but the priest's views prevailed, and Protestants realized, as never before, the benefits accruing from the Reformation.

My headquarters for a time were at Kundāpur, where, on a sandspit between river and sea, there is a brackish pond containing a large number of big fish, the scientific name of which I cannot recall but which are called Hūwumınu in Canarese. I had a great day's sport there. By ancient order no one may fish the pond without the consent of the Head Assistant Collector, and I proclaimed a fishing and got together Schmidt, the little Basel missionary, and a lot of fishermen. One set beat the water with sticks at one side, while another set, starting from the other side, dragged a big net across. Round the semicircle of the bulging net dug-outs containing two or three men ranged themselves. In each boat a man stood upright with one hand grasping the midrib of a coco-nut leaf and with the other lifting the edge of the net as high as possible. As we advanced thus, the fish began to move, and soon scores were flashing in the air. It was no easy thing to keep one's balance, smite the fish as it flew, sweep the net over it, bring it down into the boat and at the same time dodge a sledge-hammer blow in the face. Many fish leapt the net, some soaring right over our heads, but in the end we bagged seventy-two, which were laid out and distributed according to Mamool, the god of the country, and not a bad god either.

There was a report current in the district that it was customary to provide the Basel missionaries with wives by means of shipments of women volunteering for the purpose. I asked Schmidt whether this story was true. He confirmed it, and said that the system worked better than might be anticipated. He added reflectively, "Now, Mrs. Schmidt—I cannot say that I should have chosen her but she is a very good wife."

I have referred before to that noble hill the Kudiremukh, the monstrous precipices of which dominate South Canara from a height of six thousand feet and which looks eastward over the superb Malnād of Mysore. Beltangadi lies at the foot of it, and from that place, one blazing morning in March, I trudged to the base and then to the top of the smooth, black cone of Jamālābād, which rises like an acorn out of its cup to a height of nearly a thousand feet. Numberless rough steps form a pathway which penetrates encircling walls and here and there swings round cliffs with terrifying freedom. I was more than half dead when I dropped beside the little clear pool where the ferns are and the bees build. The hill had been fortified, and I marvelled to find cannon halfway up such an ascent. It is equally marvellous that such a place could be stormed. The story goes that, when the fortress in one way or another first came into our hands, it was garrisoned by sepoys under an English officer, and that that gentleman went off after bison one day and returned to find that the place had been surrendered to a party of Tippu's men. Be that as it may, for some reason or other it had to be recaptured, and I read an account of the storming of it in a contemporary newspaper which I came across in the records. A good number of lives were lost in the operation, but I forget how many.

Cherry, long ago Forest Officer in South Canara, saw an unwonted sight in these Western Ghāts. He had been out shooting and was returning in the dark when, topping a rise, he found himself looking down on a valley which from end to end was flickering with soft blue flame ; every leaf, blade, and twig was traced in fire. He tried to fix the position of this wonderful scene in his mind, and next day strove to find the place again but without success. I believe that there is some sort of phosphorescent mildew to which the phenomenon can be ascribed.

Far up northwards, in the woods against the

Ghāts, stands a small collection of huts called Kollūr, which boasted two objects of importance, a small temple and old Shaikh Haidar, the Head Constable, who wore a long beard, dyed crimson, and was a notable shikāri. The temple contained, in a tumble-down treasure-room, an unexpected hoard, comprising a flat and much-flawed emerald measuring about 3 by 2½ inches, a splendid girdle of twisted strands of gold holding several rows of large stones which were asserted to be diamonds, and a number of ornaments bearing flowers prettily depicted in enamel of a style which I have never seen elsewhere in India. The most remarkable part of the treasure was, however, the collection of cloths. There were bales and bales of exquisitely fine textures embroidered with flowers or shot with gold or silver thread. So delicate was the substance of these that the cloth could hardly be felt between the fingers. A great part of this collection was dropping to decay, for it was all very old, having been presented, as was said, by the Rajas of Bednūr, who formerly ruled in the neighbourhood. Some time after my visit thieves swooped down and sacked the treasury and only a portion of their booty was recovered.

On the plateau above is Nāgavadi, which swarms with big game of all sorts and over which towers the fine peak of Kodasādri. I passed through it on my way to the Gerasappa Falls, where, in a dense forest, a river pitches over a sheer cliff of 829 feet in height. Even at Christmastide the bungalow trembled under the shock of the cataract and in the monsoon the noise is said to be deafening. At the time of my visit the river fell in four separate streams which are known as the Raja, through whose whirling clouds of mist the pigeons and swallows fleet like drifting leaves; the Roarer; the Rocket, which descends in a shower of downward-plunging rockets with streaming, white tails; and la Dame blanche, which suggests a woman with trailing hair and vestment of lawn. The water reaches as spray a pool which is said to be 22 fathoms deep. At the bungalow were the Visitors' Books wherein travellers, inspired by the scene, had, from 1841 onwards, inscribed remarks and poems, one or two of which latter were quite good.

Striking backwards towards my own district, I turned off to visit Nagara, the old name of which was, according to the books, Bednūr, but, according to the people, Bidarūr, that is, Bambootown. It was the capital of a petty dynasty, and from the remains of a citadel can be seen a wide circle of castellated hills and the city wall. Tradition has it that the place once possessed a lakh of houses and two lakhs of wells, but the present town occupies only a small space, and of that which was old the hand of the monsoon has swept away the greater part. Scattered here and there are shrines with obscene carvings, a few reservoirs and fountains, a gateway and a handsome stone dais round a ruined Matha, or habitation of the devout. In one temple is a bell which bears an inscription stating that it was made at Amsterdam in 1713. There is, too, a small enclosure containing some rude graves of English people who died at the beginning of the nineteenth century. The epitaphs are roughly cut and full of mistakes. In one I found a certain pathos of humility: "In memory of John Clapp late a Conductor in the Hon. Company's service who departed this life 22nd September 1802. This stone was erected by Mary a woman that resided with HHim ffor eleven years."

I shall mention only one other place in South Canara, namely, Kōta. In the yard of the temple there are forty or fifty cylindrical stones which project from the ground to various heights up to two feet. This, it seems, is a natural crop, and I was told that a few years previously a number of new stones suddenly sprouted up. They are regarded as representations of the lingam (phallus), and people anxious for children anoint them with oil.

I was deputed on one occasion by the Sessions Judge to visit the jail and record a statement by a condemned murderer. The prisoner made a full confession. He and others visited the house of the victim at night and knocked at the door. The owner came to the window and, in some way or other, was induced to put his hands out, whereupon they were seized by the prisoner and another. The rest of the party then broke the door down, entered, and killed the poor wretch at their leisure. The prisoner continued—"As we were coming away from the house we saw a cock. Muttayya wanted to kill it, but I said, 'Why should we kill the poor bird? Let it alone.'" And, as another instance of the incongruity of the materials of human character, I may cite the case of a man who, when just about to be sentenced to death for murder, drew with excited concern the attention of the judge to a scorpion which was dangerously near to the latter.

While I was in the district a woman gave birth to a monster which, it was stated, had hair reaching to the feet, four eyes, and hands and feet turned backwards. When this prodigy appeared, the village elders assembled and decided that it was a Rākshasa, or demon, which would come to full stature if the wind were allowed to blow upon it. So they put a tub over it and later on killed it. Having done this, they reported the matter to the police. Greatly, no doubt, to their surprise, they were put on trial and were formally convicted of murder, but, on a report of the case, the Government commuted the sentence to a short term of imprisonment.

Perhaps I may be permitted to close this chapter with a copy of one of those quaintly-worded petitions which, from time to time, lighten the labours of every Anglo-Indian official. It is the best which I have come across, and it was addressed by an Indian subordinate on a railway to his European superior:—

"MOST HONOURED SIR,—In continuation of my telegram of the 13th instant I beg leave to bring to your notice that I had narrow escape from the attack of a Leopard by your favour and by the grace of the Almighty. A certain Leopard, I think a stray one, appeared all on a sudden to our heart-rending fear while payment was being made in the 93/7 mile on the line. Mr. Bonjour the Public Works Inspector was also with me at the time. The coolies numbered about 400. All of us were engaged. Where from and how the abovesaid Leopard managed to lie down in a fearful posture within the fencing at a distance of only 10 yards from us. The coolies, one after another, crying Tiger, Tiger took to their heels while I fortunately found a picottah standing near a ditch and got up to the top of it to save my life at any risk. Fortunately for me Mr. Lloyd the Assistant Engineer on hearing this came to the spot with three constables armed with guns ready loaded. Mr. Lloyd tried a shot but missed the aim. The constables tried one after another. In the meantime as a God-send a light engine happened to run there. The Engineer detaining the engine got into the tender and began to shoots therefrom. Aims several times failing the Leopard sprang up some of the coolies and constables wounded them by pawing them as often. In this state of things my body shook with fear as I was witnessing the trials as well as the fierce actions of the Leopard. Mr. Lloyd with the assistance of the constables had the presence of mind to shoot it undaunted with a gun brought by them till it is killed. Nearly 300 lives were saved I being one of them. Now I took heart and came down to commence payment. I herewith send one whisker and one claw of the Leopard for inspection. Begging to be excused etc. S. SOONDARARAMIAR."

With this the curtain may fall on South Canara. Years afterwards I paid a flying visit to the district in trepidation lest the passage of time should have destroyed my susceptibility to its languorous charm. My fear proved groundless. Even now and here the spell of that distant land is heavy upon me.

CHAPTER II

CUDDAPAH

THOSE who take pleasure in idleness will not despise a few hot-weather days in a British India coasting steamer such as followed my departure from Mangalore. The view of the flat shore is, indeed, uninteresting, but—*suave mari magno . . . alterius spectare laborem*—one touches at ports and watches stuff being taken off and put on, the sea is smooth, the air balmy, the food agreeable as a change, and with books and cards time passes pleasantly. At night, in sooth, a minute but vigorous ant which harbours in the berths gives the feet furiously to itch, but life is never free of some worry or other ; besides, one can always sleep on deck. I have had coasting voyages of another kind when I have been horribly ill and could tell tales of seasickness in various parts of the world, but the subject is not engaging and I will restrict myself to one.

I was on a boat running from Granville to Guernsey. The sea was boisterous, so much so that people began to feel unwell before leaving the harbour. Soon the victims were lying about in heaps. Amidst the sufferers glided a ministering angel, a young woman with a bottle of camphor drops in one hand and a bag of loaf-sugar in the other. Catching sight of a Frenchman who was conspicuous by the extremity of misery to which he had attained, she bore down on him and, holding out a lump of sugar, she began to sprinkle the liquid upon it. This proffer had a surprisingly stimulating effect. The Frenchman sprang to his feet, rushed to the open skylight, hung over it, and vomited his soul out. Beneath the skylight was a table laden with steaming viands and at it were seated the stalwarts. I was on deck. Never have I witnessed so prolonged a fit of nausea or experienced so profound a silence as at first enveloped this painful scene. It was broken by a long wailing cry from the saloon, like nothing heard on earth before or since. Then a tornado of shouts and cries, and next moment the doorway of the companion was blocked with a confused medley of struggling bodies and distorted visages. When I say that even those at rest in the scuppers writhed with laughter I shall have sufficiently indicated the poignant humour of the situation.

Strange as it seems, some persons appear to relish seasickness. I remember that the Court of Wards sent for a sea-trip a number of the young Zamindars in its charge. On their return a friend of mine asked one of them whether he had enjoyed the experience. "Oh yes, sir, thank you," replied the boy, "we had a splendid vomiting."

There was no one to receive or entertain me when at dead of night I reached Cuddapah and, lying on the station-platform there, I had my first taste of the real Indian hot weather, for, in the conservatory climate of the west coast, the temperature does not often rise over 95° in the shade. With morning I could take stock of my surroundings; the squalor and decay of the fever-smitten town and the semicircle of naked hills which concentrate upon it "those sunbeams like swords" and clutch it by the throat at night.

Moving off at once into camp, I ascended a short ghāt, descended a bit, and found myself on the Cuddapah uplands, here fenced round by a striking wall of red rock. At this point there is a small village called Guvvalacheruvu, where stood a police-station with which was associated a melancholy story which I give as I heard it. The wife of the Collector of Cuddapah was at a distant hill-station expecting a baby. In the middle of the hot weather she made a sudden resolve to return to her husband, and, on arrival at Cuddapah, found that he was away touring. She followed him as far as Guvvalacheruvu, walking the last part of the way. Then the pains came upon her, and in the police-station the lonely mother and the new-born child died. When I was there no constable would spend the night in the station-house because it was haunted by the ghost of the unhappy woman, who, with feet turned backward after the manner of Indian ghosts, wandered about wailing for her lost child.

My destination on this occasion was a wretched, mud bungalow at Rāyachōti, where I spent a rather doleful couple of months wrestling with my first Jamabandi (the annual land-revenue settlement) and an attack of dysentery. I may mention one of my "Jamabandi camps," Chākibandar to wit, because there is there a pool of peculiar properties. If you throw into it oil or leaves, they sink down to the bottom, so it is said, and, if the leaves return to the surface bearing marks of the claws of the water-spirits, it is a good omen for the thrower. My own Division was on the lowlands, over two thousand square miles of territory, mostly flat, treeless, and black ; an uninviting tract when the high millet was off the ground. It was traversed by a low, stony range known as the Yerramalais, which was classed as a Reserved Forest to the amusement of all except the Forest Officer by whom its sparse grass and occasional euphorbias were affectionately cherished. At one point the range becomes picturesque, where the Pennēr breaks through it by a fine gorge with high, ruddy cliffs on which the vultures nest in large numbers. On the edge of the pass stands a stronghold known as Gandikōta or the Ravine Fort. Mostly this place is in ruins, but there remain a grand, iron-plated doorway, a tower whence, as they say, the Nawābs of Cuddapah used to watch combats of tigers, some tall granaries on stone posts, and certain arsenals, temples, and mosques. The harem is broken down, and its deserted garden is overgrown, in tangled confusion, with shrubs and trees bearing limes and custard-apples. One wall of great height lies flat. It formed part of the powder-magazine which, after the suppression, in or about the 'Forties, of a small rebellion headed by one Narasimha Reddi, who seized the fort, was blown up, and so well was the magazine built that one wall fell in a solid, unbroken square. In the largest temple a hole will be seen in the floor ; it is said that a gosāyi dug therefrom a treasure the whereabouts of which was revealed to him in a dream.

The tale goes that, when the great Sir Thomas Munro was moving into Kurnool on the journey which ended with his death, he rode through this pass and, as he went, called attention to the yellow flowers strung in his honour from cliff to cliff. His retinue in surprise stared up into the vacant air, but an old man, wiser than the rest, whispered to another, " Soon a great and good man will surely die," for he knew that his chief had caught a glimpse of the golden blossoms with which the gods welcome an honoured guest.

I made my temporary abode in the gateway of the principal mosque, which possesses some of that grace of cleanliness and airiness which distinguishes these structures. Hard by a panther had killed a young buffalo. The body had been loosely covered with branches which sufficed to protect it all day from the vultures, but it was marvellous with what rapidity those birds collected when the branches were removed in the evening. I was a few yards off behind some stones, and within a few minutes a swarm of the filthy fowls were writhing like maggots on and within the carcass, hissing and screaming to the accompaniment of a disgusting noise of tearing and sucking. What between the stench and this spectacle my vain vigil was an unpleasant one.

My friend Tredegar, along with a companion, sat up over a goat for a panther, and it was interesting, he told me, to watch the cautious approach of the latter animal owing to the astonishing skill with which it concealed itself in a place with no apparent cover. When a few yards from the bait it crouched, and, in doing so, disappeared from sight altogether. Next moment panther and goat were rolling over and over in a wild embrace. Then Tredegar's companion took careful aim and shot the goat.

I myself saw something of this faculty for concealment. I was out on the Kudiremukh with Appu, our chief shikāri, when I caught sight of a panther (or cheetah as then and there we always called the animal), and set off after it with little hope of seeing it again. God knows what instinct taught the creature that it might safely wait for me, but I came suddenly upon it lying down facing me in grass not a foot high, at the very edge of the sheer, stupendous precipice which bounds the Mukh Head. It was perhaps ten yards off when I fired, nevertheless I missed it. There was nothing very remarkable in that. What did surprise me was the instantaneous disappearance of the beast. It just was not.

My headquarters were Cuddapah town, and for some time I lived with Ballard, the Judge, in some repute as an archæologist, in a house to which an old scandal lent distinction. It stood on the bank of a stream in the bed whereof a twelve-foot python was captured in an unusual manner. Some men saw the snake's tail wagging feebly from a hole in the bank and lugged the creature out. They found that it had devoured a litter of fox-cubs and was so swollen that it had got stuck in the hole.

Long after Ballard had got tired of me, I managed to secure for myself a ramshackle, barn-like structure built on the edge of the paddy-fields, whence in wet weather snakes invaded the building with unpleasant frequency. Often, when of an evening I entered the dimly lit lower room, shadows on the floor made unexpected and alarming movements.

Cuddapah was in those days regarded as a *locus pœnitentiæ*, and I suppose our bureaucracy was below the average in efficiency, while we harboured amongst us an uneasy-eyed individual whose scandalous life was officially cut short by an urgent request to leave the country. To our Executive Engineer, Green, who was atoning in Cuddapah for an error of judgment elsewhere, to wit, the construction of walls and a mortuary chapel for a new cemetery which he had laid out upon a sheet of rock thinly covered with soil, I am indebted for the following story :—

Green, his brother, and a third man were out in camp when they received news that there was a tiger in an adjacent millet-field. Believing that a hyæna at the utmost had been seen, they sallied forth indifferently, carrying a single-barrel rifle, a shot-gun, and a revolver. In the field the millet was lying stacked in sheaves, and amongst these was moving an animal which was, in fact, a tiger. The rifleman fired and wounded the animal, which charged and knocked him down. Green's brother fired his gun at the beast, which turned on him, threw him down, and began mauling him. A shot from the revolver drove off the tiger, which leapt a heap of sheaves, knocking over a native who had sought safety thereupon, and disappeared. Green's brother died as a result of the mauling, and, in view of that feature of the story, I can hardly doubt that it is true.

In those days Cuddapah included a large area of high upland, forming the Division of the Sub-Collector whose headquarters were at Madanapalli. Fowler, the Policeman, was stationed there in my time. One morning, when he was ready, quite ready, for his bath, he was bitten by a snake. He paused not to identify the species or to pay ceremonious observance to convention, but sped, much as he was, to a neighbour's house for consolation and advice. These took the form of a bottle of whiskey, a remedy more dangerous than the disease, seeing that the reptile was only a harmless rat-snake. However, he took down the medicine manfully, and so strong was his emotion that the quart or so of spirit had no apparent effect upon him.

Near Madanapalli there is a hill which bears the name Horsleykonda (Horsley Hill) in honour of a Collector who built a house on it. It is a pleasant place, rising solitary to a height of over 4000 feet, covered with bushes and low trees among which bears and birds abound, and steeped in peacefulness, albeit at times the air rings with the loud, rattling "Koorr-r-r—kooroop, kooroop, kooroop" of the Large Green Barbet. The bears, except in rainy weather, are not likely to be seen after sunrise, and are generally so mild that the coolies who come to the hill for forest-produce drive them off with stones, but a lady missionary known to me was treed by one, and, as the tree was thorny, it was a matter of some difficulty and delicacy to extricate her. A forest officer, too, was held up for some time by two surly specimens.

On the occasion of my last visit to this place I met there a highly-Anglicized Oriental named Pāndi, who had an interest in the habits of animals which is exceedingly rare among educated Indians. He would spend nights on the ground or in a chair hoisted into a tree watching the wild things, and asserted that he had viewed in this way the Dance of the Sambhur stags, which animals, according to him, collect at seasons and prance about before the does on their hind legs. Pāndi was one day walking along a fire-trace in a forest when a tigress, covered with mud, slipped out of the jungle into a ditch alongside the path. She did not seem to notice the men, but ran along the ditch, crossed the trace higher up, and vanished into the bushes. "It was," Pāndi observed, "just as if she had gone to warn her mate of our presence," for, a few minutes later, a large tiger walked into the middle of the trace from the point at which the tigress had disappeared, seated himself on his haunches, and in that position, looking like a huge tom-cat, quietly regarded the advancing party. The shikāri was in front, Pāndi came next, and a peon, with teeth rattling like castanets, formed the rear. The bold shikāri whispered to Pāndi to fire, but he, armed with a small rifle, counted the cost too high. The shikāri then advised a retreat backward as it would not be safe to turn, so the party stepped slowly to the rear until a twist of the path hid them from the steadfast gaze of the motionless tiger. Pāndi was informed that, at the rutting season, the tigress falls into a peculiar state, becoming, apparently, so absorbed in her passions as to be oblivious of and harmless to everything around her. The male, on the other hand, grows bolder, and cannot be intruded upon without danger.

Pāndi told me, further, of a man who was badly injured by a wild pig. While watching his crop, he wounded a boar, which charged, but, having to cross a slushy paddy-field, could not get up much pace. The man was standing on a low bank which also impeded the attack, so that he was able to catch the animal by the ears and hold it sufficiently far from him to protect his body, though his coat was cut to pieces. Finally, finding his strength waning, he made a bolt for a tree, but, as he was scrambling up, the boar struck him in the buttock and gashed to the bone, with the result that the ryot was in hospital for a couple of months.

Another story was of a man who was seized by the thigh by a tiger and flung up with such violence that he broke his front teeth against a branch, to which he clung and so saved himself.

Pāndi declared that he once came on a dead boar, frightfully torn, with the footprints of two tigers round it. A little farther on there was lying in a stream the body of a tigress, her belly ripped up by the courageous pig. I have heard on more than one occasion of boars being killed by tigers, and the Raja of Venkatagiri told me of a more singular incident. The partially devoured body of a panther was found lying by a dead cow. A kid was then tied at the spot, and next day another half-eaten panther was found there. The Raja went to the place, saw the bodies of the two panthers, and had a beat, in the course of which he shot a tigress. It is surmised that this animal found the panthers at work on the cow and kid, and, enraged at their presumption, killed and partly ate them.

Now and again a tiger appears on Horsleykonda, and for some time there was one there which was chased and harried by the two buffaloes employed in carrying water to the bungalow whenever they caught sight of it. In the end, however, the tiger took heart of grace and killed both. There was a European Deputy Collector, one W., who was a keen shikāri and singularly careless of danger. He used, it is said, to lie down beside a kill without any protection and go to sleep, trusting that the noise of the marauder feeding on the carcass would awaken him and enable him to get a shot. When this did occur, he generally missed. However that may be, this officer one night, close to his camp, wounded a tiger with slugs, and next morning he went out in pyjamas and slippers to see what had happened. He came on the brute lying under a bush, knelt down, and pulled one trigger after the other with no result, for the rifle was empty. The tiger arose and began to advance. W. had one cartridge with him ; he slipped it in, fired and missed. Next moment he was down with the tiger biting him. A Koya bravely slashed the animal over the rump with an axe. It span round and made off as the Koya shinned up a tree. The Deputy Collector was carried to Pōlavaram and put on a boat which, by the worst luck in the world, passed, on the way down to Rajahmundry, a steamer containing the District Medical Officer who was hastening up-stream to his assistance. W. succumbed to blood-poisoning.

On my last visit to Horsleykonda, after an unsuccessful beat for pigs at the foot of the hill, I sat for an hour or two in the small stone choultry talking to the Tahsildar about Hindu customs and so on, and, the subject of early marriage cropping up, he told me that one of his sisters had a child at the age of ten and a second one at the age of twelve. Both infants survived. The earlier of the two ages must, I should think, be a record. The mention of this Indian official puts me in mind of another Tahsildar in Cuddapah who carried Brahmanical pretensions to such lengths that, after the Collector had made an inspection of his office, he held a religious ceremony to purify it of the polluting aura of the European. The Collector liked this so little that he placed the man under suspension. There was a Tahsildar in Malabar who underwent a similar punishment under curious circumstances. There happened to be brewing at the time one of those Moplah outbreaks which have given trouble from time to time owing to the fanatical courage of the insurgents. The Tahsildar and the Police Inspector of the locality were both merry wags and took delight in playing tricks on one another. The Tahsildar had been the last to score, and the Inspector went off into camp "swallowing" (to use a phrase from a native newspaper) "the pill of defeat with a glum." A day or two later a messenger sent by the Inspector arrived hot-foot to warn the Tahsildar that the Moplahs had risen. Seeing in this an attempt at a counterstroke, the Tahsildar retaliated by clapping the envoy into the sub-jail and went to his rest in much contentment. Unhappily the message was a genuine one, and the Tahsildar had to pay for the time lost in consequence of his sense of humour.

I could mention one or two quaint decisions passed by our Tahsildar magistrates, but will instead refer to one attributed to a European Sub-divisional Magistrate in another Province. He had a peculiar *flair* for rape and was constantly committing men to the Sessions on this charge. As they were as constantly acquitted, he resolved to dispose himself of the next case in which this offence might be suggested. The next man, therefore, was sentenced by him to imprisonment for "causing hurt with a deadly weapon," an offence within his jurisdiction. He was in such fear, that officer, of snakes that, even in the daytime, he went about preceded by a chuprassi with a lighted lantern, and was careful to set his feet down on the chuprassi's footprints and not to shift his position if spoken to whilst on his walk.

At Mangapatnam the hills sweep round into an almost complete circle which once formed the bed of a vast tank. The railway line runs close alongside, and here, many years ago, a terrible accident befell the Bombay mail. After the disaster the two engineers in charge of the section were sought for, but they could not be found, a fact which led to their dismissal. A long while afterwards I met the senior engineer who was then in great penury, and he gave me an account of the reason for the absence of himself and his assistant. It seems that, on the night of the accident, the senior went to the house of the junior to remonstrate on his attentions to the former's wife. Remonstrances led to an altercation, blows ensued, and finally one took to flight with the other in pursuit, and it was while they were so engaged that their attendance was demanded.

My knowledge of the district is not extensive and there are but one or two more places to mention. To Siddhout, or Siddhāvattam, I went with Ballard and Wardle the Collector. The dark Lankamalais rise close by and there is a fort with fine gateways. Inside the fort are some temples and shrines which I did not examine with sufficient attention, and a pretty little mosque overlooking the river which was then beautified by the graceful forms of women bathing in clinging garments. On the way back we stopped to see the Bhōgambāvi. Steps lead down into a square structure consisting of a two-storeyed cloister surrounding a pool. Here, they say, "far sunken from the fiery breath of noon," the Mussalmān dancing-girl who gave the place its name used, two centuries or so ago, to spend idle hours swinging over the water on a bed slung between balcony and balcony. I went on a shooting trip to Bālapalli in the low, malarious Sēshāchalam Hills. A touch of fever was all that I gained, that and a memory of magical, moonlit nights when the shadows of the bamboos lay in inky bars across the chalk-white forest paths. If, however, one goes far enough through these hills, one arrives at the sacred mount of Tirumalai on which no Mussalman or Pariah may set his foot. I ascended the hill from the Chandragiri side by a steep path and rugged steps which often bore the names of pilgrims. The local band met me and a stalwart piper walked backward in front of me, making me feel like the Roman General in Anstey's story before whom marched a piper playing "Pugnare nolumus." Europeans are not admitted into the famous temple, which has a fine enclosing wall and is frequented by both Saivites and Vaishnavites. Above the temple is a large choultry where pilgrims are entertained free, and above that again is a "math" for people from the north of India. The four streets of the village form a square, and the uniformity of the houses is evidently due to their having been formed to a considerable extent by the partitioning of a cloister. The village is, in fact, a mere appendage to the temple, and the atmosphere of the place is astonishingly sacerdotal. They say that, until lately, no women were allowed to live on the hill, and that it is not very good form, even now, to dwell there with wife and family. Every one goes barefoot, and nobody should, by right, use a bedstead. As a concession, however, to the abundance of bugs and the decay of faith, it is permitted to sleep on two boxes. The place has such sanctity that even Muhammadans have been known to send, through Hindu pilgrims, offerings for the shrine.

There is good all-round shooting in Cuddapah and tigers are not rare. One of these animals was shot by Badger of the Civil Service. He had a stage put up, but one side of it was so low as to be hardly above the ground, and the whole structure was so flimsy that little pressure was needed to overturn it. By-and-by there arrived a large tiger accompanied by its mate. They were evidently suspicious, for they would not settle to the kill, but continued to roar and to roam round the machān, keeping Badger in alternating moods of amusement at their antics and terror at their proximity. Badger had a shot at the tiger and believed that he touched it, but the animals were not scared off, and continued to promenade until the tigress lighted on his water-bottle. With this she was much pleased, and began walking about carrying it in her mouth by the strap. Finally she gave Badger a chance and dropped.

I may enter here a very strange story which I should hesitate to repeat had not two persons independently assured me of its truth. At a certain public bungalow two successive watchmen had been killed by a tigress, and one B., with two friends, went to the place to try and bag her. They sat in the evening in the verandah until the others got tired and went inside, leaving B. alone. Suddenly, in the gloom, B. found the tigress by his side. She took his hand in her mouth and moved off. B., dazed by the shock, walked quietly out of the verandah alongside the animal, his hand always between her jaws. As he went the realization of his position flashed through his paralysed brain. He shouted for help, the others rushed out, and the tigress was shot.

I may end this chapter with a story which Wardle told me and which rather amused me. He was in the hill tracts of Ganjam when the Government conceived the plan of starting school for the Sāvaras or some such tribe, and, as the normal healthy man has a natural aversion to education, he was asked to pave the way for the innovation. With this object he summoned a conclave of the elders and began to expatiate on the advantages of free education. Hoping by everyday illustrations to drive his meaning into their simple minds, he went on, " Now, when the Sarkar offers you schooling for nothing, it is as if I laid a rupee upon yonder rock. If I did so, would you not take it ? " A voice answered, " No. That would be theft." Somewhat disconcerted, Wardle went on after a pause. " Well, we will put it another way. Suppose I placed a basket of eggs there and told you to help yourselves, would you not do so ? " Again a voice answered, " No. We do not eat eggs." Somehow or other Wardle got to the end of his speech, and then the leading man got on his feet and spoke on behalf of all. He acknowledged the beneficence of the Government and the excellence of their proposal to open schools, " but," he added, as definitely disposing of the matter, " the children say they won't go."

CHAPTER III

NELLORE

AFTER a short spell of duty at Madras and a journey home, I found myself at Nellore on the east coast, a mean town preserving scanty traces of the walls from which our troops had once to fall back. It is asserted that a great forest erstwhile encompassed the town and was thronged with lions, the roarings of whose ghosts frighten elephants to death, and it is a fact that there are no elephants in the neighbourhood. The European quarter, Dargamitta, is named after a group of Muhammadan tombs of which the principal one covers the remains of a saint who lost his head in battle and wandered through the world with it seeking a place of sepulture. His selection of Nellore to settle down in was not, perhaps, unconnected with the deprivation he had suffered. I shall have a good deal to say later on about the district of Nellore, but on this occasion I was there only just long enough to become embroiled with my Collector, McSweeney. That gentleman, who possessed unusual musical gifts, made himself conspicuous by his efforts to support the prestige of the Collector by jealous retention of old-fashioned attributes of office. I am far from saying that this policy was unsound, and one way and another he must have spent a good deal on the maintenance of becoming state. When the long procession of creaking carts had reached the chosen spot, the flagstaff and the numerous tents had been erected and the piano, the various beds, and other paraphernalia had been installed, McSweeney settled down for a long halt, during which his minions, on their part, busied themselves in maintaining old customs in their own peculiar way. When these traditional observances palled upon the people of the place, they would make up a purse and approach the butler, who would find some reason or other for suggesting a change of camp to his master. The mention of tents forms my excuse for bringing in here a tale of a hoax played off on an illustrated London paper. It was in the days when Lord Kitchener was Commander-in-Chief in India, days playfully referred to then by quotation of the line, "Change and d— K— in all around I see," that a humorist sent to the paper of his choice a sketch of the ordinary "necessary" tent of Indian camp-life with an explanatory note. In due course there appeared a full-page illustration of the thing under the title "An invention of Lord Kitchener," and to this was appended a note to the effect that, among the many improvements which Lord Kitchener was effecting in military affairs in India, was to be reckoned this design of a tent to replace the 80-lb. tent for officers going to the front. It was generally agreed in India that the design was more suitable for officers proceeding in the reverse direction.

An acquaintance of mine had a good deal to do with Lord Kitchener when he was employed in revising the system of military finance. At the conclusion of his job this gentleman jocosely observed to Lord Kitchener that he ought to bestow on him some military honour. "So I will gladly," responded the distinguished soldier, who apparently did not appreciate the labours of his financial adviser, "I will give you a military funeral."

Our Sub-Collector in Nellore was a Muhammadan Statutory Civilian named Wahāb Khān, a keen horseman and the only person I ever met who kept and used falcons. When the birds were in training, they were fed on the flesh of the grotesque lizard known as the "bloodsucker" mixed with red pepper and had an occasional dose of opium. Wahāb Khān described to me a chase after antelopes which ended in one of the hawks swooping and tearing out the eyes of an unfortunate animal. "It was a very pretty sight," he added. The incongruity of this remark suggests to my mind a discordant event which happened at one of the annual prize-givings of the Madras Society for the Prevention of Cruelty to Animals. At this there appeared an old Mussalmān with a hawk and a myna. He was much disappointed at not receiving a prize for the hawk, and, rushing excitedly in front of the Governor's wife who was distributing the rewards, he threw the myna into the air and launched the hawk at it. The hawk seized its quarry, and, settling in front of the lady presiding, proceeded to tear it to pieces, while the owner looked round with an air of proud confidence which changed to one of comical surprise as he was hustled out of the enclosure.

Wahāb Khān's face was that of a marauding Turcoman chieftain as I conceive such to be: lean cheeks, grim mouth and chin, raptorial nose. He said of himself in a magisterial proceeding: "If fifty Afghans armed with scimitars were to rush into my court and threaten me in the exercise of my duty, I should feel no fear," and that may have been the case. Nevertheless, some years later I saw him broken with terror shortly after he had been bitten by a mad dog and had received the visits of the many kinsfolk and friends who flocked to condole with him on his approaching end, and to describe hydrophobic horrors which had come within their experience. He survived, however, and so did W., who also was bitten at Nellore, where rabies seems to be particularly rife.

W. was sitting with others in a verandah to a post of which was tied a tame bear. A dog rushed in and attacked the bear, and the men, seeing what was toward, fled into a room. After a bit they opened the door to peer out, when the dog dashed in and fastened on to W.'s thigh with such determination that it was dragged off with difficulty. W.'s leg streamed with blood, which fact, combined with the previous tussle with the bear, may have been his saving. The bear died mad, and W. spent an awful half-year or so with the fixed resolution to shoot himself at the first sign of hydrophobia. In another instance the victim was seated one evening outside his tent in a long chair when he saw what he took to be a dog at his feet. He aimed a kick at it, and was bitten by what he then saw to be a jackal. Long afterwards (two years, as I was told), when the unfortunate man was in a remote camp in the Agency tracts, he discovered one morning that he could not bear to look at a cup of tea which was brought to him. H., who rode in forty miles on hearing of the news, was in time to see to his interment and to read the burial service over him.

I feel that this chapter would be incomplete without a tiger story, so I will give here one which I culled from a newspaper and do not otherwise vouch for. There was in the menagerie at Bangalore or Mysore a tiger which was much attached to an old keeper. One day it got loose and started to roam about the garden. The keeper went after it, and, bitterly reproaching it for the ungrateful return it had made for hospitality long enjoyed, led it back to the cage by the ear. Some time afterwards it escaped again. There was then a new keeper, who pluckily tried to repeat his predecessor's exploit with the result that he was killed.

CHAPTER IV

HEADQUARTERS

THE succeeding four or five years do not furnish much material. They were spent between Madras and Ootacamund, mostly in desk-work and burning incense to vanity. Madras, where it watches the ceaseless rise and fall of the Coromandel surf, consists centrally of a picturesque medley of houses and ramparts forming Fort St. George. Northward of that lie a large harbour and that block of straight, narrow streets which constitutes old Black Town and present George Town. Southward a stream of large public buildings, white or red, flows to San Thomé, which still in some indefinable way speaks of Portugal. Inland, if exception be made of some untidy and not too savoury clumps of huts and small tenements, the place is rather country than town, for rice-fields are found, and the spacious houses, which lower prices rendered possible a century ago, are surrounded by large tree-grown "compounds." In the so-called cold weather, when cool airs wander through the rooms and the sun irradiates scarlet blossoms and green branches in the garden, life in those houses is as pleasant as may be.

The southern boundary of the city is formed by the Adyār River on which sailing and rowing are to be got and the Theosophists have their material habitation. In Colonel Olcott's day the story went that the Theosophists had a crystal wherein the truly pure in heart and those only could see future events mirrored, and that every lady in Madras had gazed into it without catching a glimpse of anything. A hospital nurse told me that she was called in to attend a lady belonging to the Society who had been striving to emulate the fasting of Christ. She had a shanty run up on Elliot's Beach, and lay there, surrounded by admiring fisherfolk, without food or (this may be questioned) water, for twenty days. It was only on receipt from Mrs. Besant, who was in England, of a telegram authorizing, or ordering, her to discontinue her experiment that she could be induced to resume ordinary life.

Amongst my more intimate acquaintances in Madras was O'Leary, one of those harmless romancers who are so common in India and conduce so greatly to the gaiety of life. It would serve no purpose to repeat any of his anecdotes, entertaining as some of them were, and I bring him on the stage only to mention a rather neat retort to which he exposed himself. After listening to a remarkable incident in his career, a disagreeable individual observed, "That is very strange, O'Leary, very strange indeed. You would not have believed it yourself unless you had seen it, would you?" The ingenuous O'Leary, replying in the negative, received the triumphant reply, "Then you will pardon me, if I do not believe it."

Perhaps I may be permitted, while on the subject, to give two more samples of felicitous repartee.

K., one of our Under Secretaries, sued a railway company for damage done to a boxful of clothes. The counsel for the defendants directed his cross-examination of the plaintiff to securing an admission that the clothes had been over-valued. "Now look at this," he observed scornfully, holding up a coat,

"I suppose you could get a coat like this for five shillings in a reach-me-down shop, eh?" The plaintiff replied quietly, "That is a question which you are probably better able to answer than I am."

There was a subaltern who travelled from a certain place to St. Thomas' Mount and put in a bill for travelling allowance which is not permissible for journeys not exceeding five miles. He got back an Objection Memo. signed by a Colonel Bird demanding his reason for making the claim, the two places not being five miles apart "as the crow flies." The reply endorsed on the Memo. by the subaltern ran, "I did not go as the crow flies. I went on a horse. I am not a bloody Bird." The subaltern was handed up for insubordination, but they say that Lord Kitchener was so tickled by the answer that he would not do anything.

I heard of equal insubordination on the part of an Assistant Commissioner whose office management was vigorously criticized by the Commissioner, the remarks closing with the words, "This young man seems to be a past-master in doing nothing." The notes of inspection were sent to the assistant for his explanations, and against the remark quoted he wrote, "Far be it from me to dispute the opinion of an Expert in the Art."

So much for retorts and, as remotely connected therewith, a remark made by one lady to another would perhaps not be wholly out of place here. There was on board an outward-bound boat a newly wedded couple for whom it was not possible to allot a separate cabin, so the bride shared a cabin with an elderly lady. Every now and again the matron was asked to vacate the cabin temporarily to enable the husband to come in to help his wife "to pack boxes," the contents of which she had disarranged. At the end of the voyage the elder woman, taking her young companion's hand, said with a smile, "Well, good-bye, my dear. I hope that you will do your unpacking as easily as you did your packing."

The great social function of the year in Madras was in those days the Bachelors' Ball, a return for the hospitality received from the married folk. It was a matter of much preparation, for each year the entertainment was staged according to a different plan. The most successful scheme of decoration in my time was the "snow-scene" wherein powdered lime figured as snow, glass as ice, and casuarinas as fir-trees, while a lighted-up lodge and an inn with a frozen horse-trough added realism to a picture which looked uncommonly pretty and wintry under a full moon. Another good device was "The willow-pattern plate." These exhibitions of skill and fancy were swept away by a Governor who opined that the bachelors spent too much on them, and made the future loan of the Banqueting Hall conditional on the discontinuance of the scheme-system.

It was in the days of an earlier ruler that Madras woke one morning to the thrilling news that the wife of the Governor had fled from the white-columned mansion which looks over the date-palms towards the sea. The reason followed apace, and it was rumoured that more than one lady was shaking in her shoes. The details of the case need not be given. It ended in His Excellency resigning office.

The regime of his successor, a very nice fellow, was marred by a number of petty scandals of which the earliest was occasioned by a dance given by the Governor at which the women appeared accoutred as angels, while the men were in black with tail and horns complete. A harmless enough jest, one would think, but Snow, our then Bishop, a simple soul, was horrified at this onslaught upon the foundations of religion, and felt it his duty to make a protest. An absurd fuss followed in the newspapers. They say that Bishop Snow once took some ladies to view a Toda "mand" or settlement, and, in response to the usual clamour for "ilām," presented a woman with a rupee, whereupon she, overwhelmed by the magnitude of the gift, in gratitude whipped off her only garment. I cannot say that I believe this, although the Todas are certainly not prudish and sudden excitement may easily prevail over convention. A man told me that he went into the sea at Brighton to rescue a girl who was drowning. On his return with her he swam past a number of bathing-machines, and some of the women, who stood at the doors eagerly watching his progress, were apparently unconscious that they had not got a stitch of clothing on.

It was in the time of the Governor last mentioned that a visit was paid to Madras by the Czarevitch. The big ball given in his honour at Government House was so shockingly mismanaged that a friend observed to me, "Well, if the Russians have any designs upon India, this experience will be enough to keep them out of Madras at all events." I was one of those who met the Czarevitch at the railway station, where his personal insignificance was partially redeemed by a handsome uniform and a gleaming silver helmet adorned with gold. When, however, he and his staff appeared at the succeeding garden-party at Government House, attired in frock-coats and bowler-hats, we experienced a sharp drop in the respect and interest which the idea of autocracy engenders.

We young men in the Secretariat used to break our labours by a joyous tiffin at which we criticized our seniors, ragged playfully, and fed the kites which are ever wheeling and whining about the Fort. Those birds will readily snatch food from the hand, and I have seen one try to pick a cap off a boy's head. From my office window I watched a curious duel. Below was a flat roof bordered by a parapet. This parapet was black with crows all gazing intently at two of their kin, who were fighting with furious abandonment in the middle of the arena. At intervals the spectators, moved to admiration by some peculiarly shrewd thrust, would stretch out their necks and give a deep caw. Unfortunately, when the combat was at its fiercest, the birds were scared away by a man coming on to the roof.

We are not accustomed to associate chivalry and that cheerful vagabond the crow, but perhaps do him an injustice. I was witness of the following scene. There were a hen and chickens in the road, a crow exploring the flowers of a Gold Mohur tree, and a poising kite. The kite swooped and missed a chicken. The crow looked up, took in the situation at a glance, and made for the kite with such fury that the bigger bird fled. The crow then returned to its tree. I have traced altruism lower down than the birds. On the wall of a room a "chunam-frog" settled itself and began to make free with the succulent store of insect-life which had gathered near the wall-lamp. Now it is settled law that the collecting-area of each wall-lamp belongs to a particular wall-lizard. The rightful owner in this case was a small specimen which, sauntering towards supper, stopped stupefied at the sight of an intruder. Recovering from the first surprise, the small lizard began to advance very slowly towards the frog; then, deciding against a frontal attack, it took a circular route to the rear of the interloper, and, moving with caution, made a feeble peck at the batrachian's stern. Then it scurried away. On the adjacent wall was a big lizard feeding behind its own lamp. Seeing what had happened, the senior came racing from its post, threw itself upon the frog, seized it by the haunch, and flung it to the ground. Then it made its way back to its own preserve, leaving the young lizard to the undisturbed enjoyment of its rights. Once, when I was riding along a road, a ball of feathers in violent commotion fell by my horse's feet. This resolved itself into a kite and a crow locked in a frenzied struggle, and the crow was having the worst of it, the kite tearing out its feathers in bunches. The kite's appetite for combat sated, it released its enemy and settled on a tree close by. Thereupon that gallant crow, wounded and half naked, rose into the air and pitched itself at the foe. The missile smote the kite full and square in the breast and knocked it backward off its perch, and, by the time the kite had recovered its senses, the crow had disappeared.

I permit myself to give two more anecdotes concerning this great personality.

Hatfield saw a crow trying to get a bone from a vulture. It employed all sorts of ruses, including tweaking the big bird's tail and trying to whip the bone away when the tormented dignitary turned. Failing in these efforts, the crow flew off and returned with two others. Then, while one pulled the vulture's tail, the others slipped in and got the booty.

C. threwa pellet of bread to a crow, which swallowed it. Then he prepared another pellet containing some corrosive sublimate. The crow picked this up, rolled it about a bit in its beak, cast it aside, and, as a measure of precaution, proceeded to bring up the previous pellet.

I cannot think of anything in Madras particularly worth seeing except Chisholm's happy combination of Gothic and Southern Indian styles which forms the General Post Office and some of the mortuary sculpture in St. Mary's incomparably ugly church in the Fort. Within more or less easy reach of the capital there are, however, several places which deserve mention.

One of these is Tirukazhukunrram, a few miles from the hill-girdled tank of Chingleput. To this eminence a pair of vultures daily wing their way from distant Benares, and there is to be found on it a mantapam, or pavilion, hollowed out of the rock, in which, two or three centuries ago, Dutchmen from a neighbouring settlement wrote up their names. Hard by the rock is scored with deep grooves which are said to have been made by the fingers of countless sufferers from headache who first rub the stone and then their heads. From the top of the hill there is a good view of a typical Tamil pagoda of the larger sort which stands near the foot.

The general plan of such edifices is a high-walled quadrangle, or "nest" of quadrangles, and the centre of each wall is pierced by a large gateway encased in, and surmounted by, a huge storeyed structure, oblong in horizontal section, with sides sloping to a narrow ridge, in fact, roughly pyramidal in outline. These great pylons, which are locally termed gopurams, are made of stone below and of brick and plaster above, and are profusely decorated with big, outstanding figures which may represent deities in various attitudes or grotesque monsters or, perhaps, studies in flagrant indecency. If there is a succession of walls round the temple, the gopurams diminish in size as one goes inwards. In the quadrangle, or innermost quadrangle, is the small holy-of-holies rising into a cupola or into a comparatively low gopuram, and entrance is given to this central shrine through a sort of hall with solid walls and a flat, stone roof supported on pillars. The central enclosure may contain, also, subsidiary shrines, a tank, and, especially, mantapams, which are open structures formed of flat roofs supported by pillars. The form of architecture is trabeate, the arch being foreign to this, the so-called Dravidian, style. The main portions of the Southern Indian temples are, as a rule, considerably more modern than the main portions of our cathedrals, many dating from the sixteenth and seventeenth centuries, though, no doubt, in such cases the kernel of the temple is much older than the great pylons and walls which encompass it.

Another place to be seen is Māvallipuram or Māmallapuram, more commonly called the Seven Pagodas, though the edifices really number more than seven. I started down the Buckingham Canal in a house-boat in the evening, and found myself at daybreak alongside the bungalow on the sandy shore where stand the pagodas. These temples are supposed to date back to the seventh century, and so are among the earliest standing religious monuments of India. They are further remarkable because they are all incomplete, because most of them are monolithic shrines carved out of huge rocks *in situ*, and because, although based on Buddhist forms of architecture, they are adorned and arranged for the uses of Hinduism. In addition to the temples there are to be seen, carved on rocks, two great friezes of which the more famous is known as Arjuna's Penance. The figures in both of these works are considerably above the Southern Indian average.

Close to Madras the Governor's house at Guindy stands in a considerable piece of unreclaimed jungle, such, probably, as was abundant around Madras in the days when it was possible to see a tiger between the town and St. Thomas' Mount. In this park, as it is called, are wild pigs and hosts of birds of all sorts, and it is said that panthers occasionally visit the place. The long, white-columned building, as seen from the park, looks on a hot day delightfully cool and refreshing, and at night, on the occasion of a ball, when the house is bedecked with hundreds of tumblers of oil containing lighted wicks, the effect is extraordinarily pretty.

On St. Thomas' Mount, just mentioned, stands a long, narrow, low-vaulted Catholic church of the early sixteenth century. On its walls are pictures hardly to be matched for badness. The Little Mount boasts the footprints of a megapod St. Thomas and a church beneath which is a cave wherein service is held at certain seasons.

I happened to be passing through Madras a day or two after the occurrence of the great fire in the People's Park and got particulars of it from C. who was an eye-witness. A wooden enclosure containing booths, "pandāls" and so on had been put up for the purposes of a fair, and somehow or other a fire started there. A wild panic followed, and, between burning and crushing, four hundred and two persons perished. One poor wretch got his turbaned head through a hole in the paling, and, while he was shrieking for help, a heartless thief outside was seen to quietly remove the turban and walk away with it. C. said that the sight of the fleshless hands and feet sticking out of masses of writhing bodies and the stench of singeing flesh made him actually vomit.

CHAPTER V

THE PĀLGHĀT AND CARDAMOM HILLS

THIS chapter will contain an account of some shooting-trips made from Madras. In two successive years, in company with my friend Hopley, I visited the Pālghāt Hills in Malabar, our purpose being to do some shooting and to cross over the summit of Kannādikombu, which rises to 6,600 feet above the sea.

I still remember the dull misery of the first day when my unconquerable will drove my sweating body, enfeebled by months of office work, uphill, hour after hour, through stifling bamboo-brakes and across patches of slippery, sharp-edged grass. Three days of toil, enlivened by an occasional shot at an ibex, as we call the Nīlgiri wild goat, brought us to the foot of the principal peak. A party was then sent on in advance to clear a path, and, after following this and elephant tracks for three hours, we reached the point at which cutting had ceased. There a meal was eaten in the jungle amidst rain and mist, and we started to hack our way up a fearfully steep, conical hill. The summit reached, we strove to force our way along a remarkably sharp ridge, but so thick was the undergrowth that it took an hour to make a furlong. By that time darkness was coming on, so we returned to the top of the cone and pitched a small tent. Rain fell dismally, yet there was no water to be got, and, although we offered some of our beer to the coolies, they refused it. It was an uncomfortable night for all, and must have been particularly unpleasant for those capital fellows, the Malsars, as they shivered behind leaf-screens. The collapse of my cot awakened me to another sodden day. We were unable in the mist to discover our whereabouts and consequently the direction to be taken, and, therefore, reluctantly retraced our way to our previous camp, missing by good luck an elephant which turned off the narrow track just in time to avoid a meeting. All Hopley's burning words were inadequate to dry the tent sufficiently for portage by the coolies, but they ran us up at our old camp huts of boughs, leaves, and grass, which were quite artistic but a bit cold and draughty. A couple of marches carried us to the plains, where Hopley deserted me after some crisp criticism of the weather and the shooting. I reclimbed the hills, and finally found myself at Yeluvāl, where I got an ibex. Between the immense cliffs of this place, the huge flanks of Kannādikombu, and the great rock of Wadagiri there lies a valley which, for my own information, I named the Enchanted Valley. It is filled with forest of a hundred tints and the voice of a hidden waterfall.

The following year we two made another attempt upon Kannādikombu. On the first day of this expedition I really thought that I should die on the hillside betwixt cramp and faintness. However, I struggled up to Kuramalla at 4,500 feet, and, when we reached the bungalow, Hopley, rubbing his hands briskly, called out, "Now, boy, bring the beer." "No beer, Sah; done leave behind." "What? no beer!" shrieked Hopley. "Then I shall go to bed;" and, so saying and refusing the solacement of food, he flung himself down on his cot. Now and then I glanced up from my dinner to find his eyes fixed moodily upon me, his thoughts being evidently far away with the beer. Next day we climbed a high ridge in a shrieking wind and came to a precipice of great height and a fine show of rocky peaks and sharp glens full of trees. I missed a stag in the evening, and next day we got to Yeluvāl, where we camped in a spot sheltered from the monstrous wind which raved all night through the valley. Christmas Day and its successor were spent in unsuccessful expeditions after ibex. Then, marching light, we dipped into and crossed the Enchanted Valley and climbed up to Wadagiri. During that march Hopley groaned without cessation. So much I remember, but why he thus played a part usually reserved for myself I have forgotten. We camped there in a "shola," or spinney, near a swamp trampled by elephants. It was a wild spot and, being perhaps 6,000 feet above the sea, very cold at night in spite of camp-fires. We had to cheer ourselves as best we might on the following day of gloom and rain with the grand outlook upon the deadly Attipādi Valley and the tumult of hill and wood between us and the enormous bulk of the Nīlgiris.

Next day was spent by the coolies in jungle-cutting and by us in shikār, which resulted in an ibex for Hopley. Its successor started with a long wrangle with the coolies, who wanted to turn back at this point. Twelve of them were finally shamed into pushing on by the spectacle of Hopley, livid with rage, hoisting a load on to his own head and starting forward. So, leaving most of the things behind, we advanced to the conquest of the summit. At 4 o'clock, while the rest halted to pitch a camp, I went on with a Malsar and some others, and, after heavy cutting for over two hours, we struck the end of the pathway which we had made the year before, operating from the other side. It was now apparent that we had encamped on that occasion on the proud head of Kannādikombu itself and that the route over the summit was clear for the morrow. So both of us to bed with much satisfaction. Together came the breakings of day and of the intelligence that the coolies had brought with them from the last camp rations for two days only instead of four. That this was done on purpose is probable, for the fact was that the coolies were afraid to cross Kannādikombu because the smallpox goddess Māriyammāl makes her sanctuary there. Anyhow progress was effectually barred, and we returned moodily to Yeluvāl, where I saw a bear which I failed to get near. A long march brought us next day to Pālghāt, where we parted, and I hope that, if these lines should meet the eye of my very good friend and ofttimes hospitable host, he will forgive my little jokes about his reactions to the troubles we experienced together.

The mention above of ibex reminds me that MacCulloch, the planter (I can see now his long beard streaming over his shoulder as he drives his horse amain in the Ooty Hunt), had a narrow shave of being shot as one. He was out after the animals with another man, and posted himself behind a rock beyond which his beard projected. His companion saw the beard waving in the wind, thought that he had a fine saddle-back in view, and fired two bullets at it.

That gentleman would tell me over the billiard table of his experiences, and I recall a few unusual sights which came in his way. For instance, he once lighted upon the dead body of a tigress which had been bitten through the head, evidently by an animal of the same species, and again upon a tiger lying on its back and waving its legs about with the apparent object of attracting some sambhur which were standing, at gaze and stamping, not far off.

But more curious than these was his glimpse into the shark-world of the Red Sea. The episode began with passage across an area covered with floating masses of some red, jelly-like substance, and then the ship entered the realm of the sharks. There, far as the eye could reach, the sea was bristling with countless fins. Of all colours and sizes and some gigantic, the fish lay awash, so inert and lethargic that they would barely move to give the steamer way, and it took quite a long time to traverse their domain. It is surmised that they had been feeding themselves to bursting point on the red stuff previously seen.

As for myself, in my many voyages I never saw a shark, but I saw something more beautiful and not vouchsafed to many in that same region between the gaunt bones of Aden and the haggard mountains which stare down upon the Gulf of Suez. That was the star-shower of November 1885, and it wove a lacework of glittering threads across the face of the High Heavens. Is not it in Malabar that they account for shooting-stars in this wise? When a cobra comes upon a hoard of buried gold, it coils itself up on the spot and stays there until the gold has condensed into a diamond of surpassing lustre. By this time the serpent is exhausted by its long fast, and, taking the jewel in its mouth, it flies through the air to restore its vigour by a bathe in the cold waters of the northern seas. We see it going and returning and miscall it a shooting-star.

In the expedition to the Cardamom Hills of Travancore I had Lascelles for my companion. We started with a long railway journey to Ammayyanāyakkanūr, followed that with a day and a half in bullock-coaches, and wound up with a seven-mile walk uphill which brought us to Tekkadi. We were now in the Cardamom Hills, which form a western wall to the district of Madura, a territory still described as " the Pāndya Country " by the hill coolies, though " King Pandion is dead " and has been so for many long centuries. On foot and by boat we passed to Periyār Camp, where stands the great dam which waters part of Madura. At that time the irrigation scheme had not been completed and the dam was only 105 feet high, considerably below its present altitude ; nevertheless, it had already formed a pretty lake winding among wooded knolls and covering some fourteen square miles.

Shortly before our arrival a ghastly accident had happened at the camp. One of the European engineers fell into a pit where a circular saw was working, and, before it could be stopped, both his legs were off. Another accident which proved trivial occurred about the same time. A cooly fell over the edge of the dam into the rocky bed of the river. The dam has a slight slope, but it was little short of a miracle that he escaped with some bruises and scratches after a fall of over seventy feet.

The completion of this great irrigation work fell to the lot of a Royal Engineer, Colonel Pennycuick. I knew him well. A man of much ability with a vivacious, deeply furrowed face. The enthusiasm with which, in defiance of malaria, the engineers working on the project devoted themselves to their duties was a testimony to their chief's qualities as well as to their own. The high tension at which he lived was amusingly illustrated when he was playing games, for then, if things were going ill, he might be seen, in a frenzy of excitement, tearing his handkerchief or shirt-sleeve to shreds with his teeth. It is said that Colonel Pennycuick once fell under the high displeasure of the Government. He had been ordered to prepare a scheme for supplying some town or other with water from a certain river. He reported briefly that the levels did not admit of the project being carried through and the Chief Engineer told him, in reply, to obey orders and not to raise frivolous objections. Colonel Pennycuick's response was that, while, as regards the scheme in question, he was unable to alter or add to his previous report, he would be happy, if so directed, to propound a scheme for carrying water from the river to the town *by train*.

This flippancy led, as I heard, to suitable punishment which did not, however, prevent Colonel Pennycuick from rising ultimately to the rank of Chief Engineer, and, while he held that office, the administration of the police was in the hands of the stern and capable Colonel Sloggett, who also in earlier days had incurred the dire wrath of the Government. The opinion then expressed regarding Colonel Sloggett was a grave doubt whether he would ever be fit for the duties of a police officer and whether he should not be returned to his regiment in disgrace, and the occasion for this censure was his burning down somewhere in the wilds a village where a dacoit was supposed to be harbouring with the connivance of the villagers. In this act, which, with mud and thatch huts concerned, was much less drastic than it sounds, Sloggett was abetted by a Civilian whom I used to see in later days limping about with a lame leg. I was given the following account of the origin of his lameness. A panther had been caught in one of those huge mouse-traps which, baited with a goat, are set for such animals. The beast was turned loose in the presence of three men who tried to spear it.

As a result the man I have mentioned was bitten in the knee, whilst another Civilian was so severely mauled that he died. This latter was an ardent whist player. When his end was near, the chaplain came to pray by his side, and to his earnest intercession the dying man seemed to be paying equally earnest attention, but, at the finish, he only observed in a faint voice, "You ought to have finessed that Queen." An unexpected remark which carries my memory back to a tale of an unexpected remark on the part of the Civilian Spedding, a merry fellow in his day. He attended a mission meeting somewhere in England, and heard an orator declaim hotly against the manners of Europeans towards the inhabitants of tropical countries. At the close of the speech Spedding rose and craved the privilege of a few words on the strength of long acquaintanceship with India. He admitted and deplored the tendency alluded to, but urged that of late years a marked change for the better had taken place in India, "so much so," he concluded, "that no European now thinks of addressing a native without prefixing the honorific title of *suwar* or *bāhinchut*." He sat down amidst applause on the part of those members of the audience who did not understand the two terms.

Colonel Sloggett, to revert to that gentleman for a moment, had sufficient sense of his own value and dignity to face a Governor openly. There was a young police officer Turner, and Mrs. Turner was attractive, and the Governor was supposed to regard her with paternal benignancy. A vacancy occurring in the post of Superintendent of Police at Ootacamund, the summer headquarters of the Government, Sloggett submitted a proposal for filling it. Through his Private Secretary the Governor thereupon asked whether the Inspector-General did not think that

Turner would be a suitable substitute for his nominee. Sloggett's answer was that Turner was wholly unfit for the post. The Private Secretary then wrote that His Excellency had nevertheless decided to give the appointment to Turner. Sloggett replied that the decision rested with the Governor, and that, when gazetting Mr. Turner to Ootacamund, the Government should also gazette his own resignation of the post of Inspector-General. Needless to say, Turner did not get Ootacamund, and the Governor of that day was a man who would appreciate Sloggett's attitude rather than resent it.

I have rambled a long way off the track through the Cardamom Hills, but, as the police have just been under mention, I crave permission to repeat, before returning to the line of march, a story which used, I believe, to be rife in Northern India.

It was shortly after the Mutiny and hot chase was being made after a notorious dacoit with whom a long score had to be settled. It was known that he was visiting his native village X. because his wife there had become pregnant and had not been outcasted. The Police Superintendent of District A. was a smart man, and he disguised himself and some of his men as Sanyāsis, or religious mendicants, and went to X., where day after day they sat in meditation by the tank with an eyelid lifting for the dacoit. News of this gathering reached the Superintendent of District B., a rival smart man. Convinced that the Sanyāsis were in fact the dacoit and his gang, he, with some of his men, assumed like disguise, and squatted down alongside the tank of X. There for a time the two parties remained passive, each satisfied that the dacoit and his companions faced it. At last moral certainty became conviction with the B. Superintendent. He sprang on his prey, and in the course of a severe struggle the mutual error became revealed.

And so to ourselves. From Periyār Camp we moved northward through as pretty a bit of country as I ever saw. Elevation perhaps 3,000 feet. Around us, undulating alternation of forest and of grassland bearing growth high as man. To the north the High Range. To the south the ridge of the High Wavy Mountains, so named from an old map whereon that bit of country is marked " High wavy mountains covered with dark and impenetrable forest." This description of the range still applies, I believe. B. got lost there, and spent a night in the jungle tormented by leeches and harassed by a prowling elephant. Next day he and the Brahman with him made their way to the plains by a march of twenty-seven miles. I do not know how the Brahman sustained himself, but B. had a fowl which had died of exposure, and on that, raw or half cooked, he fared with little gusto.

We saw many bison as we went along\but did not secure even one. Lascelles, indeed, wounded a bull, but we lost track of it after following it for a couple of hours. I watched for a time a small herd feeding close by me, the bull having made off. Handsome creatures they are with their great black bodies and white legs. Twice or thrice we came upon elephants, and, although the shooting of them is unlawful, we followed one herd with the intention on the part of Lascelles of getting a shot at a tusker, which, however, proved impossible. A bear and a stag were sighted, but neither gave a chance, so, in the end, the expedition failed of its purpose. The nights were mostly spent in huts constructed with astonishing skill of grass and the leaves and stalks of the *īta*; one of these contained as many as five rooms. At Udamānshola, whence a striking view of the High Range is to be got, there is, however, a bungalow which has a moat round it to keep off elephants, and here there live a few people who made their presence known towards evening by great screaming and drumming for the benefit of a roaming tiger.

From this place we tottered on strained and aching legs down a fearfully steep path to the plains. We breakfasted under a banyan, toiled four weary miles of sandy track to Kombai, famous for its breed of black-muzzled dogs, travelled by cart to Uttama-pālaiyam, and so reached the railway at noon of the following day.

Lascelles is responsible for the following instance of unusual pertinacity of anger on the part of a bison. He had wounded the animal, and was apparently following it up when it charged him. He fired and leapt to one side. The animal missed him, stopped itself abruptly by ploughing up the ground with its hoofs, wheeled round, and came at him again. This time a horn ran through his clothes between shirt and skin, and the beast went on at a gallop with Lascelles hanging from one horn in much fear of being dashed against a tree. After he had been carried in this way for about a hundred yards, the clothes gave way, and he fell to the ground uninjured. while the bison passed through a clump of bamboos as if through a paper screen and disappeared.

It was in the Cardamom Hills that Douglas of the Public Works Department had his singular experience with a tiger. He was in an *īta* hut with three rooms, in one of which he slept while the coolies occupied another, and the third was used for stores, which included some ducks and fowls. In the night Douglas was awakened by a tremendous hubbub, and found that a tiger had entered the hut and dragged out a cooly whom, scared by the din, it left badly mauled close by. An hour or so later the animal came back and carried off a fowl. Then it returned for a duck. After this Douglas tied up a goat and sat watching by a hole in the wall. The goat was seized almost at once and Douglas shot the marauder. The brute's condition indicated starvation, and it was said to be a well-known manslayer. I think I heard also that the animal's state was due to its fangs having grown into the palate.

A planter from Travancore told me of a peculiar method of destroying tigers which is practised in that country. The rāgi plant (*Eleusine coracana*) is twice cut down before seeding ; it is then allowed to bear seed of which a paste is made. This is rubbed into the body of an animal killed by a tiger, with the result that, when the tiger feeds again on the carcass, it becomes stupefied and is easily disposed of. I have no other authority for saying that rāgi so treated has narcotic properties.

The same person told me of three Travancoreans who were attacked by a tiger while walking in single file through the jungle. As they were passing along, number 3 saw the animal preparing to spring on number 2 and shouted a warning. Number 2 jumped to one side, with the result that the tiger missed its objective and fell sprawling on the path, and, before it recovered itself, number 3 brained it with an axe. I can give other instances to disprove the assertion of the Bengali writer that under English rule the inhabitants of India have become "a timid herd of quill-driving sheep." Lascelles came unexpectedly upon two bears which made for him. One he shot and the she-bear turned tail. As she went off, Lascelles wounded her in the rump, whereupon she swung round and attacked him. His cartridges jammed, and he gave himself up for lost, but three of his shikāris, armed with spears, sprang between him and the enemy, and scared her away by shouting and leaping about. Again, Lascelles saw three men go down into a deep, dark hole after a bear. They found it, and one of them fired a revolver in its face and got badly hurt as a consequence.

CHAPTER VI

BELLARY

AFTER a period of long leave I found myself *en route* for Bellary, labelled as a Judge.

Bellary was described by a private soldier with an eye for topography and a limited stock of epithets as "just two bloody rocks." These rocks are two of those tors so common all over the Ceded Districts and Deccan generally; vast masses of stone split into enormous boulders which cling to the parent stock in wild confusion. Often they are belted and helmed with walls and citadels which speak of vanished chieftains and old marauding days as emphatically as do the *burzulu* or towers of refuge which are found in so many villages in these inland parts. Such craggy hills have a peculiar charm of changing colour, from black, through gray and rose, to violet, according to the will of "the Queen of colours, Light," and the ancient strongholds they bear delight the eye with their blocks of fallen masonry among a tangle of bushes, their rough, stalwart walls and their massive gateways, all bathed in the lucent air of early day.

One of the Bellary rocks is known as the Face Rock, because, from certain positions, it reveals the semblance of a gigantic face staring at the sky. The other bears an interesting fort with the customary intricate maze of stout walls winding amidst boulders and clinging to sloping sheets of rock. Here for a time was confined in recent years the ruler of a native State who was believed to have murdered his wife. Not far off is the jail, where hangings used to take place in a secluded spot just outside the premises, and the Superintendent told me that on more than one occasion he had known European ladies of the station to put in an appearance for the pleasure of witnessing an execution. The black soil of Bellary, betwixt the scanty rains and the hot weather, becomes soft and powdery and affords excellent riding. The Cantonment at that time was an unkempt place, with mean bungalows and bare, untended compounds. The station was reckoned healthy, that being before the invasions of plague and malaria.

The only place outside headquarters visited by me is Hampi, the first capital of that Vijayanagar dynasty which for a long while dammed the flood of Muhammadan invasion. The locality is now very feverish ; a rocky country through which the Tungabhadra rushes and eddies. The small temple of Vitthalaswāmi there is richly carved, but, on the whole, the remains of the city are disappointing. The ruins cover a considerable area, but are, for the most part, of little account in themselves.

At Bellary I came across Gellibrand, an author and a person of vast erudition. He began his literary labours, as I heard, before he went to the East with a convincing work on the Indian Frontier Problem, concerning which book a reviewer remarked that it revealed in every line the writer's intimate personal knowledge of the region under discourse. Some years later he produced an amazing volume on the Irish Question which he proposed to settle on ultra-Cromwellian lines. Suggestions made by him when he was consulted as to the amendment of the Code of Criminal Procedure, were not less drastic. He advocated the establishment of "Courts of Honour" to determine criminal proceedings between Europeans and Indians. In these courts evidence was to be valued arithmetically. Starting with the sound enough premiss that the testimony of a cooly is worth nothing at all, he generously valued it at unity. There followed an ascending scale of values which closed with the word of the English gentleman rated at, we will say, one thousand. Thus judicial decision was simply a matter of addition and subtraction. On the general principle which should underlie criminal legislation in India he held decided views, and in the course of his essay, which he printed and distributed freely, he argued for a free hand for the European in minor matters; "why," he asked, "should not an Englishman beat a nasty, dirty, greasy denizen of the bazaar?".

If rumour may be trusted, Gellibrand's passion for cricket led at times to an interchange of catches between Bench and Bar during the progress of a case, and even to brief adjournments, when bewildered witnesses were impressed to field at a knock-up game while pavid litigants shrank at the wicket from the incomprehensible and frantic efforts of the Judge to injure them with a ball. But perhaps the predominant trait in this gentleman's character was his horror of the Indian as a possible carrier of infection. I myself noticed that he would not touch furniture with his bare hand, for fear lest the servant who cleaned it should in doing so have contaminated it with some disease, and I heard circumstantial accounts of the consequences of a peon picking up his cricket-bat by the handle. In order to emphasize the enormity of the offence, the culprit and all the other retainers were summoned to form a burial-party which escorted the infected bat into the garden, where, by lantern-light and with great solemnity, it was interred.

Speake, the Banker, is another person whom I may mention. He was intensely interested in Oriental magic, in which he fully believed. It was reported that in his own person he could perform one of the simpler feats into the grotesque details of which it is unnecessary to enter. He once met a Yōgi who professed to have power to kill by willing. Speake tried to get him to perform on a dog, and was taunting him about his reluctance to do so when a mangy cur appeared on the scene. The gardener threw a stone at it and it fell dead after running a few yards. Of course the Yōgi claimed the honour, but Speake showed proper scepticism over this. With full measure of belief, however, he assured me that he saw, on the bank of a tank, a Hindu devotee rise from the ground in a sitting posture and remain so, suspended in the air, for several minutes. Be that as it may, I must ask the reader to give credence to my own experience.

In the notes on Chapter LXI of Yule's edition of "Marco Polo" will be found a reference to a few early cases of levitation in India and a statement that an exhibition of the same on the part of a Madras Brahman was reported to have taken place a few years before the date (1874) of the book. I can claim to add another instance to Colonel Yule's scanty list, and I never met anyone, except my companions on the occasion in question and Speake, whose testimony is discounted by his tendency to mysticism, who professed to have witnessed in India a case of floating in the air. The exhibition took place in 1887 at Periyakulam in Madura, and I made a note, an all-too-scanty note, about it at the time. My note shows that the exhibition took place about 4 p.m. The Guru, a thin young Brahman with a haggard and clever face, was put into a square tent and seemed to fall into a trance ; at least his eyes were shut. He rested one hand lightly on the top of a stick and remained stretched out horizontally in the air ; the stick was removed, and he remained, resting his hand on another man's hand, touching it lightly. We got him to do this twice, and passed sticks under him and found nothing. The performance took place in the open. The Guru was naked save for a loin-cloth when he entered the tent, but was covered with silk cloths which almost reached the ground when he reappeared in a horizontal position some three or four feet from the ground. My *recollection* is that the tent or canopy was the flimsiest of things and that it was entirely removed when the floating figure was revealed, but my memory surely plays me false on that point. There must have been some form of suspension. Yet it escaped my notice and I cannot pretend to explain the feat.

That is the only good bit of "magic" I have seen in India, but Eyre saw a clever trick at Bimlipatam. A., B., and C. were Telugu Brahmans of whom B. and C. professed to know no European language. Eyre said a sentence in German to A., who knew English. A. then went over to B., who was standing out of earshot of C., and repeated the sentence, as best he could, to him. B. then walked across to C. and began moving his eyeballs in various ways, C. meanwhile watching him intently. B. did not move his lips. After a somewhat long interval C. repeated aloud the sentence which Eyre had spoken to A. with some natural modifications but in an intelligible form. Similar success was obtained with sentences in Latin and Greek. It would seem that a code had been arranged whereby certain movements of the eyes represented certain sounds, but it must have been a difficult code to read.

CHAPTER VII

GŌDĀVARI

I WAS but a few months in Bellary but my Judgeship at Rajahmundry in Gōdāvari lasted only a few weeks, so that I must resort to extraneous matter to make up a chapter about the District.

I occupied a large house on the bank of the noble river, and this building I associate very hesitatingly with an anecdote which I heard long ago. A certain Collector received a visit from a wealthy Zamindar, who sought a favour at his hands. The visitor was received in a verandah overhanging the river, and came accompanied, as is usual enough, by a tray containing some limes which form the visiting-card of India. The tray was put down beside the official, who, as conversation proceeded, began fingering the fruits, which struck him as remarkably heavy. Satisfied that they were golden presentments intended as a bribe, the Collector said nothing, but, as he sat and talked, from time to time he idly tossed one lime after another into the deep water alongside, while the Zamindar watched in futile anguish the gradual disappearance of his princely gift.

Some years after my time a popular outbreak occurred at Cocanāda, the headquarters of the district, a quiet, sleepy place which is being left high and dry by the retreat of the sea. It arose out of the impertinence of a schoolboy and his consequent thrashing by the European affronted. This incident was worked up by those interested in causing trouble until a mob collected and besieged the English Club. The Collector was wounded in the face by a soda-water bottle used as a missile, but I do not remember whether there were any other casualties.

In Madras itself, at one time, deliberate efforts were made by an emissary from the north to stir up disorder, and large crowds used to assemble on the beach to hear this orator breathing out threatenings and slaughter. Beyond demonstrations by noisy mobs, nothing much ensued, but the situation might easily have developed into turmoil and loss of life, and the Government were severely criticized for a supineness which was, I believe, dictated to them from England.

Things were much worse in the Tinnevelly district, where outbreaks, partly due to local causes, at Tinnevelly and Tuticorin had to be put down by force. One night, at the latter place, things looked so bad that the European women and children were put on a steamer, while the men assembled at the Bank. The populace had a strange belief that the Japanese, as champions of Asiatic interests, were coming to their aid.

The alarm created by the situation in the extreme south caused an uneasy feeling in neighbouring districts. I was warned that secret, seditious meetings were taking place at Srīrangam, but disbelieved the news, and that town and Trichinopoly, where I was then stationed, remained quiet in spite of the circulation of a pamphlet advocating the murder of Englishmen. It was, however, somewhat suggestive of popular sympathy with the rioters of Tinnevelly that the Superintendent of Police at Trichinopoly was unable to get any of the pensioned sepoys living there to take service as punitive police in Tinnevelly, the offer of tempting emoluments notwithstanding. So much for the very brief record of disturbances directed against Europeans in the south during my time.

Among the much more common riots of a non-political type one occurred at Guntur. The real reason for it did not appear in the correspondence. I was told that it arose out of the molestation of some women. Several people were killed and an unhappy constable was burnt alive by the furious mob. The outbreak was badly handled, the Parsi officer in charge of the division failing in nerve. The principal police officer was an Indian. The District Magistrate described in sarcastic terms how the latter rode, "slowly I am afraid," towards the scene of conflict and, having arrived, got, "or fell," off his horse, flung off his uniform, rushed into a building, and hid himself under some sacks. One of the constables who was questioned about the occurrence made a rather amusing remark. He described himself as lying half dead through injuries he had received when somebody came up and struck him a heavy blow on the head with a rice-pounder; "this," he proceeded, "revived me."

The worst "domestic" conflict in my days was the Shānār-Maravar outbreak in Tinnevelly, which almost approached the dimensions of civil war. The Shānārs are the local toddy-drawers, and growing prosperity has induced them to put forward claims to religious privileges which are resented by the higher castes. The Maravars are a somewhat barbarous lot, and useful tools in the hands of those who want violent deeds done. It was said that they were instigated on this occasion by certain Zamindars to bring the Shānārs into a state of mind more befitting their position. Whether this was so or not, the

Maravars took this task in hand and attacked a Shānār village, where a regular massacre took place. The Government were dissatisfied with the conduct of the District Magistrate, whereupon the Judge took command of a party which supported that officer and set itself in opposition to his successor. To end this curious feud the Government had to transfer several European officers. That Judge and a Revenue officer, working in opposition, had previously split official Malabar into two factions, which discharged such floods of corrosive ink that the quarrel reached the Secretary of State at last, and resulted in a very proper rebuke to the Madras Government for allowing matters to go so far.

Forming a special group are the periodical Moplah risings in Malabar which, commonly originating with grievances against Nāyar landlords, take the shape finally of rebellion against infidel rule. Three or four of these occurred in my time. The first resulted in the death of some thirty of the rioters, whose courage, as always, commanded respect and raised regret for the cruel necessity of their death. In the penultimate outbreak ninety-six Moplahs perished. During this very serious disturbance the district was in the charge of a gentleman not easily to be disturbed from the even tenor of his ways. I was told that his imperturbability and indifference to the agitation at Headquarters preyed cruelly upon the spirits of His Excellency the Governor in Council.

I am tempted to give in this miscellaneous chapter one or two extracts from native newspapers. The first is a sample of the sort of comments upon the Boer War which were to be found in the baser organs of the Press.

" The British people . . . are now moping like owls. . . . They are being crushed like oilseeds in a machine. They . . . are being kicked even by dogs. Lord Kitchener who was soundly beaten, kicked and crushed by the Boers, is now sitting quiet with his glory dimmed and his mind confused and is incessantly calling out the names of Jesus and Mary. . . . General French who had on many occasions run away from the Boer force . . . had 5000 soldiers with him while . . . General Botha had but 200 men. The battle lasted for six hours. . . . The dead bodies of these people appeared like a hill, their blood ran like a river, and the wild dogs and foxes . . . began to prey upon them with great joy. Seeing this horrible sight, General French said to himself, 'If I remain here for a minute more, I shall certainly lose my life. . . . What does it matter to me whether the British or the Boers rule over the Transvaal? I fight only for money.' So saying, General French fled away . . . and none was able to overtake him."

Another passage, which is taken from a Ceylon newspaper, describes a little-known episode of the Russo-Japanese War. It runs:

"The Sultan was communicated with regarding the approaching conflict and, being a great friend of the Japanese Emperor, sent a specially trained company of swordsmen, each of whom with a sword in his hand is shot away from the mouth of a gun at the enemy like ordinary shrapnel. On arrival among the enemy he makes short work of them by his swordplay. These swordsmen are now fighting for Japan and gaining victories."

I return to the district which supplies a heading for this chapter in an anecdote supplied to me by the Collector of Gōdāvari. Among the Collector's elephants was a cow of irritable disposition. She had been annoyed by being compelled to haul a boat out of the river, and, when she was afterwards required to pick up something for the mahout, she refused to do so. Thereupon the man hit her on the head with an axe. Forthwith she set herself to shake him off and, succeeding in doing so, made attempts to gore him while on the ground with her small tusks. Two other mahouts hurried on their animals to the rescue and were charged by the cow. The dismounted mahout seized the opportunity to get on his feet and make for the river. The elephant, returning from her pursuit of the would-be helpers, began looking about for her enemy and caught sight of him. She strode into the river, overtook the wretched man as he splashed and floundered in desperate efforts to escape, snatched him up in her trunk, and returned to the shore with him. There she laid him down deliberately and squashed him by kneeling on him. Strange to say, the sight of this dreadful deed threw the other two elephants which had returned to the scene into such a state of excitement that they made an attack upon a neighbouring village, whence the people swarmed out with cries of terror. I suppose that the other mahouts had slipped off, for the three animals then went away into the jungle, and they did not return to their quarters for several days.

CHAPTER VIII

COIMBATORE

FAMINE and other pressing demands upon the Civil establishment in Bombay led to my going for a short time in a judicial capacity to Dharwar in that Presidency, but I find it impossible to furnish from that episode material for a separate chapter, so shall treat it as merely introductory to my spell of service at Coimbatore. The town of Dharwar stands on the tableland which forms the core of the peninsula of India, and its nearness to the coast moderates the temperature, while the south-west monsoon makes itself felt only by a current of cool air and drifts of fine rain. So it is an agreeable enough spot, and sufficiently in touch with the wild for a panther to kill a calf in my compound. The calf was close to the house, but the marauder stayed to make something of a meal. Panthers are often astonishingly bold. I will illustrate this remark by the experience of a planter who one night was roused from sleep by a blow in the back which almost threw him out of his canvas cot. What had happened was seemingly this. There was a dog tied to a leg of the bed. A panther sneaked into the room towards the bed, and the dog retreated from it as far as its tether would allow. The panther crouched under the bed to spring, and, in leaping, brought its back up against the bed. The shock alarmed the animal as much as the man and it bolted.

I met a man who killed a panther with his bare hands. He was a fine specimen of humanity and the panther had been previously wounded, perhaps badly. Anyhow it had strength enough to fling itself upon him, and he got it by the throat with both hands and throttled it, but was severely clawed in the process.

Almost the only incident which stands out in my memory in connection with this station was a visit from the Governor of Bombay, and that only because it furnished an opportunity to an enterprising thief who was in unobtrusive attendance upon the gubernatorial party, to deprive of his belongings the police officer who was on guard over His Excellency's person and property. One can well believe that to a depredator of sporting instincts the belongings of a policeman are an irresistible attraction. There was an Assistant Superintendent who was after a gang of thieves in Madras, and in the course of the chase spent a night in a public bungalow. Some of the fugitives entered his room and removed all his property, and in addition, as a vaunt, all the furniture of the room down to the hat-rack, with the exception, of course, of the bed on which their pursuer was sleeping.

On the way from Dharwar to Coimbatore, to which district I had been posted as Collector and District Magistrate, my wife and I halted at Bangalore to stay with Colonel Allen. That officer had been a brother subaltern with Sir Richard Burton, the traveller, and he supplied several stories about him which were new to me. Burton was not apparently popular with his messmates, towards whom he adopted, according to my host, an insolent and overbearing attitude.

Allen had been a keen shikāri, and I will repeat one or two of his sporting reminiscences.

On one occasion he wounded a bear which was

tracked into a cave. The native shikāri jocularly dared Allen to go in after it, and Allen, little as he liked the job, liked less to refuse the challenge. So, grasping a spear and lying flat, for the cave was low, he proceeded to wriggle inwards, the shikāri worming behind him. Eftsoons there was a grunt and a shuffle, and a bear lurched heavily towards the orifice over the bodies of the two sportsmen. This was an unwounded animal, for, when Allen a minute later pulled up against some hair, it was luckily found that the owner of it was dead.

Another story is more remarkable. Allen and his wife, when in camp somewhere in the wilds, went off for an excursion on a cow-elephant. They had just finished their tiffin when a tusker appeared on the edge of the jungle, and, as it showed a disposition to join the party, Allen got his wife on to the cow, and they started to return to their camp, the bull following them. Between the two animals walked Allen carrying his rifle, and, whenever the bull showed signs of a disposition to come too near, Allen would stop and raise his rifle. Then the tusker also would stop, shake its head, and look at the man with imploring eyes. This interrupted march continued for about five miles to the confines of the encampment. There the pertinacious suitor definitely halted, and Allen, seeing its peaceful attitude, walked right up to the animal, which passed its trunk over his head and turned quietly back. Much to Allen's distress, for the great creature's conduct had evinced a benignant dignity of disposition, a man hurried up from the camp at this juncture and shot the bull dead.

So we fared to Coimbatore, which desirable district lies below the Nīlgiris ; possesses at Pālghāt a vast ventilator through which, during the south-west monsoon, pours the fresh wind from the sea without its rain; and includes a large area of rugged hill country in the north and the great and noble Ānaimalai range in the south.

Arrived here, my first care was to furbish up my Tamil with the aid of old vernacular correspondence, and, in doing so, I lighted on the strange fact that subscriptions were collected among the natives of this district for the benefit of European sufferers in the Mutiny, various clerks and others being shown as contributors. Whether this was a spontaneous ebullition of pity on the part of the Indian population or a result of pressure on the part of the Collector, I cannot say. A step outside Coimbatore town is Pērūr temple, which possesses well-carved pillars, statuary of a comparatively superior quality, and that mystery of darkness and dim twinkling of lights which give a certain solemnity to the larger Dravidian temples.

That place left far behind, I arrived at Mountstuart, some 2,000 feet up in the Ānaimalais, where I came across Eyre the Forest Officer, who was then toiling to make a success of a scheme for establishing a saw-mill on the hills. At that time the wire ropes for carrying logs down to the plains had been erected. As a trolley filled with wood went down, an empty one came up, and coolies would take advantage of this means of ascent although the line soared to dangerous heights. One man, going up in this manner, found, owing to some obstacle in the way, destruction imminent, leapt out on to the top of a tree and saved his life at the cost of a broken thigh. Eyre had a bison-calf which became so tame that it would enter his bungalow and thrust its great hairy head over his shoulder when he was writing. A planter whose veracity I had no means of gauging told me that he became possessed of a full-grown bison which he kept for three months in a pen and that in a few weeks it showed obvious enjoyment of "mālishing," or rubbing-down, and soon allowed its owner to get on its back. Ultimately it broke loose and went off with a herd.

Eyre's calf was caught in an elephant-pit. So was a mouse-deer which I kept for a long time, though it was the most uninteresting creature imaginable. It was about ten inches high, stood always on the tips of its hoofs, and, despite the prettiness of speckled hide and slender limbs, looked the fool it was. It never became in any degree tamer, and would dash itself wildly about in its hutch, if approached, to the extent of making its head bleed. It ate only one sort of food, and that was *withered* leaves, a proof that its habitat is high forest where nothing green is to be found near the ground.

There is around Mountstuart (a place low enough to be deemed very feverish) a mighty forest haunted by large butterflies in regal costume of white and velvety-black and by handsome black-and-yellow spiders, an inch and a half in body-length, which spin notably tough webs. I went into the heart of this forest, pitched a tent under its immense trees, and tramped its mournful depths in search of bison, which I came upon when suffering so much in temper and body through weariness that I failed to get a shot. Finding that the roughness of the country rendered passage across the mountains very difficult, I descended to the plains, and made my way to Punāchi (4,500 feet) by a steep bridle-path called the Prince of Wales' trace, because it was made for King Edward, when Prince of Wales, who designed to make a shooting-trip into this country, but was thwarted by doctors, who scented cholera somewhere in the neighbourhood. The trace was laid out by a Royal Engineer named Law, who had a genius for aligning mountain-roads.

His fame was spread over the Presidency. Even on Funk Hill, on the Kudiremukh, the guide would point to a small rock at the edge of that sharp grass-slope which drops to an abyss and describe how Law would stand on his head there and wave his legs in derision of danger. Macey, who knew Law, said that his agility and skill in balancing were extraordinary. He could walk round a mess-table on the top back-rails of the chairs, run at a wall and take three steps up it and, with the aid of knees and shoulders, wriggle up the corner of a room (presumably the walls were not quite smooth) until he touched the ceiling.

There was an old man called Reubens, a retired Indian Civilian, who boasted that in his early days he, too, could make three steps up a wall and also vault a billiard-table lengthwise, taking three steps on it on his hands, and supported his statement by displaying a book in which allusion was made to his "astonishing acrobatic feats." Nor was this old gentleman averse to recalling the practical jokes with which he had flavoured life; quite good some of them were, for he was a merry soul, but considerations of space forbid rehearsal of them. As Assistant Collector Reubens was in a district close to Delhi during the Mutiny. His duty was to tour about and try to collect revenue. Four companies of sepoys were attached to him as a guard and he went in constant fear of being murdered by his protectors ("I was always a funky sort of chap," he observed). In course of time this force got reduced to fifty men through desertion, and, when a sepoy departed, he often sent a playful bullet through Reubens' tent to scare him. "Why they did not do for me," he remarked, "I don't know. I suppose they must have thought me a bit cranky, and perhaps they were right."

But to resume. From the Punāchi bungalow, perched on the side of a hill, there is to be got a great panorama of the rocks and lawns of the higher mountains which overtop even the Nılgiris and exalt their varied and beautiful crests to a height which nearly touches 9,000 feet. In familiar words—

> "Those solemn peaks but to the stars are known,
> But to the stars and the cold lunar beams.
> Alone the sun arises and alone
> Spring the great streams."

Leaving Punāchi after a vain search for game with some Kāders, those jungle-folk who file their front teeth, I walked for four hours to Pāralai in the almost continuous shade of high trees, the finest bit of forest I have seen in India. So I reached land which was being opened up for tea-planting, and it was enough to make one weep to see the monstrous trunks which had been felled and left to rot.

My next tour took me to Bhavāni, whereby the river Kāvēri, crossed by a railway bridge of twenty-six spans, flows among innumerable rocks. I embarked upon it in a small round coracle of cane and hide and, seeking for a shot at a crocodile, danced and span down it for some distance. As I remember, there was a full moon that day, and in her light the commonplace temple of Bhavāni took on such magical beauty that the picture of it remains with me.

A couple of marches and Tāmmarakarai was reached. There one is at an elevation of 3,500 feet and on the plateau which occupies the north of Coimbatore, a rough and shaggy region. At this particular spot are to be seen underground cells composed of flat stones, which locally bear the name "Pāndyan houses," and are reputed to have been occupied by a race of dwarfs. The country northward of this place is almost entirely uninhabited and by no means healthy. On my way across it I stopped to secure what was alleged to be a panther but was, in fact, a jackal seen against a dazzling sunset, and in three or four marches reached Kollegāl, which is not far from the fine Biligarangan range, and is principally known for malaria and the cultivation of the silkworm.

There I picked up Stark, my Assistant, and we travelled together to the Sivasamudram Falls. A long narrow bridge crosses the Kāvēri at that place. It is made of slabs of stone laid on rough stone uprights, and the builder got a grant of land for the perpetual maintenance of this primitive structure. The river forms two falls. In the case of the eastern arm the higher part of the river-bed sweeps round into a horseshoe, and into the arena so formed the river drops between two and three hundred feet by numerous streams. In the case of the western arm the main current makes two leaps of the descent. It is a striking bit of scenery, and the sanctity of the spot is attested by the presence of several temples. At that time there were, apparently, no permanent residents, the place being very feverish.

On return to headquarters I had to deal with a summons issued against a clergyman for an alleged assault upon his milkman, and that is not the only case which has come to my notice where ministers of religion have resorted too readily to temporal means for the castigation of evildoers. None of these, however, showed such vigour in chastisement as a lady, who in all apparent seriousness sought my advice as to the legality and expediency of buying an airgun for the purpose of shooting persons trespassing in her compound. I felt, however, that she was already sufficiently equipped for the battle of life when I heard her describe how she ended an argument with the milkman over the quality of the milk. One of her husband's peons, too, by a theft of currency notes brought himself within the field of her activities, and her brusque action leading up to, and following, the discovery of the missing property in the man's turban puts me in mind of a search conducted elsewhere.

When Tredegar was Chief Presidency Magistrate he had to try a case in which a person was charged with introducing contraband goods into the Penitentiary. The defence being that the strictness exercised in supervision rendered such introduction impossible, he went to the jail to see exactly what was done in the way of searching people entering the place. Enquiry showed that every precaution was taken, but Tredegar was not satisfied with verbal assurances, and directed the jailor to give him an exact representation of the mode of search. The party were within the jail premises at the time, and the jailor, to exemplify the completeness of the method followed, turned to a warder standing beside him and snatched off his turban. Down fell a cascade of that prohibited article, tobacco.

I had occasion once to hold an enquiry into a rather serious riot which had occurred at the Penitentiary, and was somewhat amused by the remarks made by two of the convicts about the matter. One complained bitterly that, by reason of recent occurrences, the jail had ceased to be "a respectable place," while the other demanded liberation on the ground that the place had become a "battlefield," and added that it was his intention, if released, either to live quietly with his brother or to devote himself to attaining salvation (mōksham).

By the way, to revert for a moment to the clergy. The wife of a member of that body suffered to an unusual extent from the nervousness which affects some people when occasion brings their near relatives before the public. In consideration of this weakness, her husband had given her a promise that he would deliver only written sermons. One day, however, he forgot to bring the manuscript to church, and with horror Mrs. Cushion saw him preparing in the pulpit to preach *ex tempore*. When he started, this feeling developed into a spasm of physical nausea which grew until, in a few minutes, she was fain to rush out of the building retching loudly. Few, perhaps, have been affected to quite that extent by a sermon.

West of Coimbatore town lie hills, and Dixon the Executive Engineer asked me to visit them with him to search for a source whence drinking-water could be drawn for the town. So, accompanied by Stark and B., we went up the Bōlampatti Valley and climbed its steep southern wall. The top of this wall forms a very narrow ridge which is in regular use as an elephant-track, and may, as Stark suggested, be called the Grand Trunk Road. On the farther side of the wall, grassy slopes dip into wooded dales, beyond which the land rises to form the great mountain mass which culminates in the challenging cone of Kannādikombu. Over the edge of the wall we had grass huts made and tents pitched.

On the following morning we started along the Grand Trunk Road with no very clear notion of Dixon's plans, but happy to find such a delightful locality so near to headquarters. A little way along the ridge we came upon a spongy mass, forming the afterbirth of an elephant, and then upon the still-born calf with a caul over its face. The little creature was perfectly formed, and had evidently been dropped but a very short time. Noting that the place would not be an agreeable one for a meeting with an elephant, we passed on through grass higher than ourselves. We were out all day, and it was evening when we got near the dead calf again. Below, to the right, was a holt in which we heard elephants. Wishing to get a view of them, we stole down the hill, and had reached the wood when we heard a trumpeting, a crashing, and the voice of B. singing out from a tree, "Look out. She's coming at us like smoke." I heard Stark drawl, "Is it a case of bolting?" to Dixon, whose answer was to clear a bush like a deer. That pair were over the ridge in a flash. B. had descended from his tree, but what exactly he did with himself afterwards I do not know. Meanwhile I was making rather rapid progress when I found myself on the edge of a cliff. By me was a small, forked, withered tree. Behind this I prepared for the final struggle, which looked hopeless enough when I found that the cartridges had dropped out of my rifle and that I had no others with me. But we had all crossed the crest of the ridge by now, and, on losing sight of us, the elephant lost interest in the chase or else she preferred to devote some attention to my dog, which was afterwards found trembling in a corner of one of the huts. The elephant was, no doubt, the mother of the calf, and was lying up to avenge its inexplicable death. We had not done with her yet.

That night I was aroused by a loud "toot," followed by a whirlwind of yells and tremendous clashing and clattering of frying-pans and kerosene-oil tins on the part of our servants and the Irulars. I poked out of my tent a dolorous face. "What the devil is the matter?" It was answered that we were undergoing an attack by the elephant, so I joined the group stationed within the circle of light thrown by the fire. The progress of the animal in the encompassing blackness was indicated by spirts of Tamil, "Pār, Pār, ang' irukk'adu," "Varukk' adu, varukk'aḍu," "Ayyō, ayyō," and, at each wild cry, crash, crash, went the sticks on the kerosene tins. It was a moving scene and had highly picturesque elements. But, when a smashing in the wood alongside showed that the animal was retreating before the noise, the disappearance of the spectacular properties of the situation caused me little regret.

In the course of the resumed explorations of the following morning our guides, who had for some time been scouting warily ahead, announced their opinion that we were on the heels of an elephant, and that it was a dangerous rogue well known to them. B. was for pushing on, but the general opinion was in favour of a halt for tiffin, to give the animal ahead a good start. At the close of the meal, the guides were not satisfied that the beast had cleared off the path, and, after some debate, we resolved to return. On the way back, Dixon proposed to make a wide détour to inspect another part of the country for a water supply, but, when this was suggested to the guides, they took exception on the ground that the tract swarmed with elephants. Moved by pity for their fears, Dixon put forward the proposition that we should return to our camp, and this was carried.

I stood outside my tent next day and watched the dawn spread her allurements over the hills. Through the pale and scentless air there stole a radiance ; in the dark, dew-drenched thicket alongside a jungle-cock woke with a cry of joy ; low down an unsuspected wisp of cloud blazed into gold. Half an hour later we were stepping briskly homewards under a burning sun.

I should have had much more to say about Coimbatore had I not, with a suddenness which aroused my high indignation, been directed to make for the Central Provinces to do duty there as a Divisional Judge.

CHAPTER IX

THE CENTRAL PROVINCES

IN comparison with the towns of Madras, Jabalpur is clean and orderly. The climate becomes quite bearable with the advent of the south-west monsoon, but for a couple of months it is abominably hot, and almost worse than the heat of April and May is the daylong, nightlong, raving crescendo of that Hawk-cuckoo which goes by the appropriate name "the Brainfever bird."

As a touring judge, I had to hold assize at Raipur and Bilāspur as well as to sit at Jabalpur, and the little I saw of the Central Provinces I liked, though I was always chafing to get back to Madras. Of two places which I visited, the Marble Rocks and Pachmarhi, I may give some particulars.

At the former place, the proper name of which is Bhēra Ghāt, the Nerbadda runs between marble cliffs which rise perhaps seventy or eighty feet above the river when it is low. In the rains, I was told, the stream in the narrowest part at times actually overflows these banks. In places the cliffs are stained, but elsewhere they are almost as white as snow. The winding gorge alters incessantly in form and width with the movement of the boat and, where the river contracts to twenty or thirty yards between its shining walls, the scene is one of haunting beauty. But it is needful to beware of the bees. People have been killed by them ; rash smokers in boats, persecuted until they took to the water, and then so harried, when they put their heads above the surface, that drowning resulted. I remember a military funeral at Madras being broken up by a swarm of bees. The vibration of the drum or of the bell is supposed to have annoyed the insects, which attacked the party at the grave. The ensuing scene resembled a football match, and a lot of people were badly stung. Some of these were quite ill for days, diarrhœa being a prominent symptom.

Pachmarhi, in the Sātpura range, is the sanitarium of the Central Provinces. It is only about 3,500 feet above the sea, but that means a drop of some ten degrees of temperature. The place is pretty, too ; a park-like plain encircled by sandstone hills culminating in 4,500 feet at Dhūp Garh, which means, I suppose, House of Sunshine. The truly remarkable feature of the locality is the rifts or earth-cracks, known locally as khads. Every here and there the ground has split into very narrow clefts with sheer sides. How deep they are I wot not ; perhaps five hundred feet, perhaps more. I went down one of them, Fuller's Khad. It was terribly hot work, but the toil had its recompense at the bottom in a luxuriant growth of tree-ferns and a deep, delightful, blue pool. From one point five of these great cañons spread like the rays of a star, and the poetry of the English race has found for it the romantic appellation, "Fleetwood Junction." From Pachmarhi I went to see a big cave near the picturesque peak Mahādeo. The cavern is sacred to Siva and was in old days a famous place of pilgrimage. There the pious left the instruments of torture with which they had vexed their route, and very business-like things these are. Beds studded thickly with sharp spikes two or three inches long, sandals bristling with points of more moderate size, spits to run through the cheeks, and heavy iron bars to be used for the same purpose and to be carried between the aching jaws. There were numerous other unpleasant articles which testified to the reality of devotion in former days. Manifestations of religious emotion are more restrained nowadays, but I have seen a man measuring his way along the ground —with extraordinary rapidity, up and down, up and down—and another with an uplifted arm which had presumably been fastened in that position until, at the expense of what agony, it had withered immovably so. Again, I saw an ascetic in hospital at Srīrangam who, fearing lest carnal temptation should some day overpower principle, had mutilated himself in such a way as to leave desire unaffected while rendering its assuagement impossible. There was the root of the matter in that man. A person I saw during the Dasserah festival at Trichinopoly rolling over and over in the road was probably only on the look-out for alms. Upon his hands he balanced the lid of a basket in which lay peacefully an infant, and the man was marvellously clever in so manipulating the cradle by a circular movement of his arms that the child lay undisturbed at the same level all the time.

I was struck by the simplicity of the Civil and Criminal work in the Central Provinces as compared with that arising in Madras, where the enormous elaboration of perjury is an outstanding feature. In the happier Central Provinces of those days the accused, if guilty (and perhaps, sometimes, if innocent), confessed or, if he did essay a defence, made a very clumsy job of it. At Raipur I was trying a young Muhammadan for some offence or other when I noticed a constable wrench something out of his hand. Immediately afterwards there was an outcry just outside the Court, and, on my demanding the cause, an old man with a long, white beard was brought in and declared that the police had been beating him for handing something to the accused, who was his son. This something was what the constable had snatched from the prisoner, and it consisted of two bits of twig wrapped in paper. These, after spells had been uttered over them in a graveyard, formed a charm potent to protect the holder from misfortune, and, in handing the packet to his son when the trial began, the old man had done what he could for him. The spell worked in fact, for the case ended in acquittal. Two of the various murder cases which have come before me I particularly remember ; one because of the criminal's description of the monstrous, shadowy shapes which hung over him counselling to slay ; the other because of the horror in the voice of the old woman who described the victim staggering out of the house of slaughter with his head wobbling about on his half-severed neck.

Perhaps I may as well continue from this point with a few judicial reminiscences of a trifling character, for I have little more to say about the Central Provinces.

An impudent attempt was once made to befool the Madras High Court. The plaintiff was a gosha woman and the defendant, a young man, cited her as a witness. She was brought into Court in a closed palankeen, from behind the curtains of which she squeaked evidence so wholly detrimental to her case that suspicion was aroused. Therefore the curtains were drawn back and the bashful form of the defendant was disclosed.

I think that it is to somewhere about this period that one must assign the once-famous Noakhāli Judgment. This lengthy document, of a character unique in judicial records, was penned by a talented Civilian, who, after a varied career, found himself posted as Judge to Noakhāli. He considered, apparently, that he had been badly treated, and, in his resentment, he seems to have laid himself out to obtain what I have seen described as "the Right Worshipful and Very Ancient Order of the N.O.K." An opportunity for this was found in a criminal case committed for trial to his Court. The judgment was retailed in sections by the daily papers, "for an enraptured public to muse on over its matutinal muffin," but unfortunately I have to depend upon my memory for an account of it. The case under consideration was first disposed of with contemptuous comments upon the conduct of the prosecution, and the Judge then turned to general matters. He began with some remarks upon the qualities and pedigree of the then reigning Viceroy, and, having brought down that rocketer, he turned his attention to humbler game. The qualities of the Lieutenant-Governor, under the *soubriquet* of "Soapy John," were discussed, the financial transactions of certain High Court Judges were touched upon, the Chief Secretary came under criticism for receiving the writer "in his shirt," and the efforts of the Executive to overawe the Judiciary were exposed in an anecdote of a dispute between the Judge and the Deputy Commissioner over the right of one to graze a pony in the other's compound. Having launched this judgment upon the world, the author of it gave himself leave out of India and went home. Every one was much interested as to the line which the Secretary of State would adopt, and we all felt it to be a disappointing evasion of the real issue when he dismissed the Judge from the public service on the merely technical ground of absence without leave.

The Code of Civil Procedure contains a sensible provision which authorizes settlement of a dispute in accordance with a test which both parties accept as conclusive, a provision which might usefully be extended to certain minor criminal offences. Tredegar saw an interesting example of the working of this clause somewhere in Ganjam. The presiding officer of the Court led the parties to a gloomy pool in the jungle. The plaintiff was young and lusty, the defendant an aged man, and, as the test was to enter the pool and keep head and body under water as long as possible, the odds seemed to be on the former. But there was this peculiarity about the tarn that the party who was lying would, on immersion, surrender himself helpless into the talons of devils who swarmed in the water. The old man walked boldly in, planted his stick and disappeared from view. The youth had hardly dipped his nose when he let forth a wild scream and came splashing to the shore, where blows and revilings awaited him on the part of the spectators.

Probably few people in England have any idea what rural life in India really is, of the dissensions which rend villages asunder, and of the foul conspiracies and crimes to which these factious quarrels give birth. The acuteness of the enmities engendered may be gauged from the fact that I have heard of a mother dashing out her baby's brains in order to bring heavenly condemnation upon an enemy (an example of the idea underlying the strange and now prohibited practice of "sitting dharna") as well as from the following incidents. In a village of Coimbatore Faction A. had been so continuously predominant over Faction B. that the latter had become reduced to the person of one old woman and her son. The mother brooded deeply over the misfortunes of her party and formed a heroic resolution. Summoning her son to her side, she informed him that, as she had not long to live, she proposed to sanctify her end by a powerful stroke at Faction A. She therefore adjured the youth to kill her, and so dispose of her remains as to ensure suspicion falling on the enemy. It was, of course, to be his further pious duty to see that oral evidence was forthcoming to drive suspicion home. The son, after some argument, accepted the sacred trust, killed the stout old partisan, and made so fair a case that certain members of Faction A. found themselves committed to the Sessions Court on a charge of murder. There, however, an unexpected witness turned up whose testimony resulted, I believe, in the son being put on trial and convicted. Again, in a village in Madura, there were two parties involved in a struggle *à outrance*, and, the time having come in the opinion of Faction A. for vigorous action, they commissioned a certain C. to procure a person who might be murdered, without risk to themselves, in such a manner that, with fair semblance of probability, the death might be laid at the door of Faction B. The commissary called in some friends to help him, and they discussed ways and means and cast about for a suitable victim. An unknown wandering beggar who chanced to be touring the locality was selected, the choice was ratified by the party-leaders, and the beggar was duly killed by C. and his mates. The next step was that C. laid a complaint before the police to the effect that the beggar was his own nephew, and that he had been done to death by Faction B. The resulting investigation went, however, so ill for the conspirators that C., who had, perhaps, been treated too parsimoniously, was brought to make a full confession.

Our subordinate civil judiciary in Madras have a tendency to long-windedness in their decisions, but are industrious and intelligent. One of the cleverest members of that body whom I have met was a District

Munsif named Krishna Rāo, who wrote in English a play called "Chandrahāsa," a copy of which he sent to Tennyson. The poet acknowledged the gift with the remark that he had never seen anything like it before, which ambiguous compliment gave the liveliest satisfaction to the author. The play was really quite a respectable production for a man writing in a foreign language (if English can be called a foreign language in respect of the educated South Indian Brahman), but I recall no detail of it save a funny stage direction. The heroine, in frantic grief over something, shrieks her intention to dash out her brains and rushes off the stage; then comes the direction "(dashing of brains heard within)."

Print supplies my recollection with other unusual scraps of English. I saw, for example, in the *Bystander of India* the remark, "We believe that Lady Hardinge has a warm heart under her petticoats," and, in an Indian novelette dealing with the adventures of a man disguised as a woman, the crisis at which the revelation of sex took place was described in the following words: "Then she undressed her breast and stood in his trousers."

As to the written and spoken tongue a hundred deliciously quaint bits of Indian-English flit through my mind, but oh, how much more deliciously quaint bits of Tamil, Telugu, and Canarese must enliven the retrospect of those ryots and coolies who have met me!

Before, on the intervention of my very good friend the then Governor (he died soon afterwards as a result of injuries inflicted upon him by brigands in North Africa), I return to Madras, I will make mention of an episode which greatly stirred society at Jabalpur shortly before I reached the place. A leading Educational Officer there went home on leave, and he returned with a wife who, without doubt, vastly enhanced the gaiety of the station. It was altogether a better, brighter place, and, from the Chief Commissioner downwards through Generals and Commissioners, the men treated the new-comer with the utmost suavity and consideration. Alas and alack! There arrived at Jabalpur a lady who knew the Principal's wife in England, and she declared unequivocally that that lady and the new-comer were not one and the same person. Enquiries followed. The lady was found to be on a temporary footing and the audacious educationist disappeared.

CHAPTER X

THE NĪLGIRIS

OUTSIDE the valley in which lies the town of Ootacamund a wide expanse of green downland swells and sinks like a heaving sea with a multitude of balsams and louseworts to touch it to colour and strobilanthes to patch it with a plumlike bloom. The nooks and folds generally contain little woods, known locally as sholas. In these is a subdued merriment of brooks, and aged boughs, dropping beards of gray lichen, carpet the ground with a shifting pattern of light and shade. Over the downs sweeps the Ooty Hunt, sharp-drawn in a blaze of sunshine or vaguely seen through a shroud of fine rain. There, too, on gray mornings of fitful brightening, the blue swallows hang, almost within hand's reach, motionless against the thrumming wind. To the south-east the vast and rather gloomy mass of Doddabetta strives to reach nine thousand feet.

Below the northern and eastern confines of this aerial island lie the jungles of the Wynaad (the "Sickly Land") and the great, malarious ravine known as the Mysore Ditch. To the west enormous, forest-clad hillsides slope into Malabar. From the southern edge one looks down upon the plains of Coimbatore or, as often as not, upon a sheet of milk-white cloud which rolls in billows over the lower hills and tosses in stainless spray against the summit of Lambton's Peak.

So much in general terms for a locality which is favourably known throughout India for the sport it supplies in the form of jackal hunting. I was out one morning with the hounds when they swam the Pykāra river on the track of a sambhur which turned to bay on the further bank. The Master, fearing for his hounds, started, booted as he was, to swim across. Halfway over he sank and was seen huddled together in the clear water. He was dead when he was brought to the surface. The hounds often go astray after wild pigs also, and one old boar which they tackled injured nine of them before it was shot. Sometimes other game attract them off the right path. I heard that, a good many years ago, the Hunt got out a professional huntsman from England. On the first occasion on which he was out with the hounds they dashed into a shola where they gave tongue loudly. The huntsman leapt off his horse and rushed into the spinney swearing fiercely. He went in quickly but he came out faster, and, with an ashen face, jumped on to his horse and galloped away. It was found then that the hounds were baying a panther.

These latter animals are often shot near Ootacamund, and one which Moxon turned out of Doddabelta shola bit one beater through the shoulder and another through the face. Tigers are less frequent but not uncommon, even on the Upper Plateau. One was shot by a fine sportsman of over seventy close to the Ooty Club, but that was before my time. Another rushed out at a bicyclist on the Kōtagiri road, but soon abandoned the chase, being of a less determined character than the animal which, in another district, sprang at a horseman, clawed the horse, and carried on the pursuit until rider and horse fell into a nullah.

when only it was scared off by the man setting fire to the grass near him. When I was at Kōtagiri I was told that a tigress had killed a cow and two donkeys some miles off, and that this animal had been previously wounded in a beat in the course of which she had killed three beaters.

H., a planter I knew, was walking over a hill near Kodanād when he saw a tigress advancing towards him out of a shola. To account for her minatory attitude one must presume that she had cubs with her, but her courage failed before the yells and frantic capers in which H. indulged. Finally, it was on the Upper Plateau that a tiger killed our Commander-in-Chief in the days when Madras had a separate army.

Except in that instance no European fell a victim to a wild beast on the Upper Plateau in my time, and, more remarkably, I can recall only one death in the hunting-field. In that case the accident happened to a mere lad, the son of a deservedly popular Governor. The poor boy was found lying in a ditch under his horse, which was so firmly wedged in that it had to be dug out ; the rider had been smothered in the mud. After I left India, however, the veteran MacCulloch died as the result of a fall while hunting.

My duties as Collector involved touring, of course, but I was not long in the district and have not much to say about it. Coonoor and Kōtagiri are ordinary hill-stations and call for no remark. The fine waterfall at Pykāra is worth a visit, and so is Avalanche in the Kundah range, which gets its name from a landslide which occurred there a while back. There was a solitary bungalow at Avalanche which was reached by a basket slung across a stream on a rope. From the high hill behind, on a fine day, a marvellous scene is disclosed. The Ootacamund valley with its ring of hills seems to be afloat in the air and, to the southward, in splendid confusion, crowd Lambton's Peak, the Pālghāt Hills, the Nelliyāmpatis, the Ānaimalais, and the Palnis. I have heard that out beyond Avalanche a man essayed to reach Malabar by a ghāt which was entered in the military route-book of the day as "practicable for wheeled traffic." As a fact the way was overgrown to such an extent that passage was impossible, and the traveller with his servants got benighted. It came on to rain heavily and grew very cold, and the servant was so much overcome that his master took him on his back. Thus laden, he struggled on until he found that he was carrying a corpse. There was also a tale of a Chinaman who escaped from the jail at Ootacamund and made for this ghāt. He too died on it of exposure.

On the chain of the Kundahs, northward of Avalanche, stands Mukurti, a gigantic fang of rock jutting out over an abyss. From this pinnacle the souls of the dead launch themselves into their future realm of space.

The Lower Plateau, or South-East Wynaad, is a malarious stretch of forest broken here and there by an up-springing hill, and here and there by a green ribbon of swamp. At the miserable hamlet of Gudalūr I met my Head Assistant Scambler whose aptitude for languages, refreshing unconventionality, and nimbleness of mind will not be forgotten by those who knew him. After reciting to me during the progress of lunch a Provençale poem of prodigious length, he took me for a drive into the forest in his trap, and it was not long before he ran against the post of a bridge crossing a rocky stream-bed. The pony swung round against the bridge-rail, which gave way, but by a miracle the animal did not follow the broken bars. Escaping further manifestations of Scambler's goodwill, I rode to Dēvāla where were then to be found, as memorials of unsuccessful gold-mining, empty bungalows and abandoned gardens where the fourcroyas still threw up their twenty-foot inflorescences. So by a circuitous route I reached Nellacottah, whence seven elephants carried me and my things to Benne, where there were some wooden bungalows standing on piles in a forest of teak, terminalias, and bamboo. This part of the country is inhabited by Kurumbars, but most of them had fled under the impression that the object of my visit was to destroy them by inoculation, and that the plague camp which was under construction at Kākanhalla was to serve as their mausoleum.

At Benne Dallas the Forest Officer joined me, and we spent some pleasant days in wandering on pad-elephants through the Mudumalai forest. It was curious to see the indifference of the deer to our passage. They would glance up at our approach, notice only the elephants, and go on grazing again. There were plenty of wild elephants about, but we did not see any, and when I left the place on horseback I was not eager to come across them. As I have said, they do not seem to like horses. The sister of a friend of mine was riding with her husband through a forest in Cochin State. The lady, who was in front, came suddenly face to face with a bull elephant. Both the ponies whipped round and dashed off. The tusker followed them furiously. The mad gallop along the narrow forest path ended in the terrified woman falling off her horse and the elephant crushing her life out under its thundering feet.

Why we never use elephants in the south for following up wounded tigers I do not know. If any animal's help is obtained, it is as often as not that of the domestic buffalo, whose courage is not to be disputed, although I have heard of a single wounded tiger clawing and putting to flight a herd of ten. The boldness of the tame buffalo is inherited from the wild animal, which is very rare and local in the Madras Presidency. I have not seen anything of these animals except their enormous horns in the houses of old "Agency" officers. Some years ago the Indian newspapers contained an account of a deplorable incident which happened in the North. W. killed a buffalo and wounded its mate, which made off but soon returned to the side of the dead animal. W., carrying a single-barrel rifle, walked to within sixty paces of the wounded beast, which then charged. Having waited until it was ten yards off, W. fired, but he failed to stop it. The sportsman's instantaneous decision was that there was no time to dodge and that the best chance of avoiding the horns was to take the shock sideways, and, as his mind decided, his body moved. Missed by the horns but struck by the forehead, W. was flung over the buffalo's back into a wallow which was so slippery that he could not get on to his feet. The beast at that moment caught sight of a shikāri or other Indian running away and set off after him. It caught him up, passed a horn clean through him, and galloped some distance carrying the bleeding trophy. Then it shook off its burden and returned to finish off W., who was still struggling to stand up. He was quite at the animal's mercy, but at the edge of the wallow it dropped dead. I have met only one man who had been injured by a wild buffalo. In that case the animal got the point of one horn into the thigh and the other point into the cheek and tossed its enemy. His life was probably saved by his orderly, who called the beast off by firing into its rump.

I heard of a different sort of injury which was

inflicted upon a ryot by a domestic buffalo. He sold his cotton crop for five hundred rupee notes, which he wrapped in a plantain leaf and carried home. At his door he put down the packet for a moment in order to lift up a child who had fallen down, and then turned in time to see the precious parcel disappear down the throat of the family buffalo.

On my return to headquarters, I was entertained by my wife by the recital of two sermons she had heard. In the one the preacher, who affected a supposedly popular style, described a spiritual crisis in his own life in these impressive words, "Then I just turned to and prayed like Billy—O." In the other the chaplain, preaching on the text "Take no thought for the morrow," pointed his discourse by the case of the young widow of a curate who, on an income of £70 a year, was able, with Divine assistance, to live comfortably in London and at the same time to maintain a small house on the river.

The Ooty Club, pervaded by rowdy cavalry subalterns and by young planters ebullient after solitude, was, in the days before the calming influence of Bridge had made itself felt, a place not altogether to the taste of the staid and sober-minded. These young men found entertainment in playing various practical jokes on each other. Among the victims was Lipman, who was honourably known to all for the correctness of his life and the uncompromising strictness of his principles. Some of his friends penned to him a letter which was signed by an unknown female name. It begged Lipman to meet the writer after sundown in St. Stephen's churchyard. This despatched, the writers got from a milliner one of the frames on which women's dresses are exhibited, and this they accoutred in feminine attire, adding a becoming hat. The figure was set up in the churchyard and the plotters hid themselves behind tombstones. As night came on, Lipman was seen casually entering the graveyard. It was not so dark that he could not distinguish the figure and he advanced towards it, raised his hat, and began to introduce himself very pleasantly. A lot of innocent amusement was got out of pranks like this.

Of the appearance, habits, and magical powers of the interesting and decaying tribe, known as the Todas, which inhabits the Upper Plateau I shall say nothing, but, *en passant*, I may allude to their buffaloes, which are upstanding, hairy, fierce-looking beasts, very different to the ordinary buffalo of the South, one of the ugliest of created things. These Toda buffaloes are becoming accustomed to horses and rarely attack equestrians nowadays, but I have heard of a man being hoisted out of the saddle by one which got a horn under his thigh and another had the temerity to unhorse the Master himself. Personally, when riding, I gave the animals as wide as berth as possible, having had sufficient experience of the pleasures of the chase when my mare was pursued by a stallion, although I was not then called upon to rival the performance attributed to Tompkins. That gentleman, on a mare, started for a ride with Raynor on a stallion. The latter animal's first indication of excitement was to get rid of Raynor. It then started for Tompkins, who rode like one possessed, but was overtaken. In the ensuing tumult Tompkins, who had a loose seat at the best of times, found himself, to his unbounded astonishment, on the back of the stallion. The end of the affair was tame, for the stallion, perhaps equally surprised, thereupon abandoned his designs.

My acquaintance with the Nilgiris was cut short abruptly by illness, and I had to spend a long time in

England, receiving during the latter part of that period no allowances whatever. When at the end, in considerable straits, I applied to the India Office for the customary advance to pay my fare out, I received the reply that this concession was confined to persons in receipt of leave allowances and could not be extended to those on leave without pay. This struck me as a singular arrangement.

CHAPTER XI

NELLORE AGAIN

I WAS uncommonly glad to find myself at work again in the paddy-fields among the gliding, glistering bee-eaters. The district of Nellore has already been mentioned. It consisted at this time of some eight or nine thousand square miles of scrub-land and tilth of a stony and somewhat impoverished order with, here and there, patches of paddy; the whole bounded by a flat, harbourless shore and by a bare, steep range of hills attaining more than 3,000 feet. The European society was so small that it would sometimes be represented at headquarters by two or three deserted wives, and camp life generally meant long spells of loneliness and heat. Nevertheless the district has its merits. It is, or was, for the most part healthy. There is great store of birds of all sorts from pelicans and great bustards down to honeysuckers. There is also fishing to be got in both tanks and estuaries. In the Buchireddipālem temple-tank Hatfield, Baillie my Assistant, and I landed one day thirty-nine fish weighing 155 lbs., and most of these were labeo, which are not caught without some display of art, but are of no account as food. Indeed, almost the only palatable fresh-water fish is that voracious frog-eater, the murral. It deserves mention not only on this account, but also because it is endowed with a warmth of parental feeling exceedingly rare among fish. I have had a murral spring out of the water at my face when I bent down to look at the fry it was guarding.

Estuary fishing is more interesting than tank fishing by reason of the waywardness of the sea-fish, or, rather, our ignorance of their habits, and pleasanter by reason of the swirl and sparkle of the tides and the breeze off the sea. In this, as in all other sports, our leader and adviser was Hatfield. I saw that officer once hook a Brahminy kite. A live bait was being used, and the bird, swooping at it, got a foot entangled in the hook. It took some time to bring the kite ashore.

A salt-water canal flanks the coast of Nellore from north to south. Walking alongside it, one disturbs hosts of mud-skippers, which run out of bushes down to the water's edge and go hopping over the surface like frogs. It is hard to realize that they are fish. On the sandy spits at the river-mouths armies of calling-crabs switch from left to right their one big, white claw with a simultaneity which passes comprehension. In the shallow water beside them lie parrot-fish, with swollen belly upwards; on alarm these balloons convert themselves into pencils and slip away. There are sure to be gulls about and perhaps a white-tailed eagle looking about for an osprey to despoil. Such were our companions at our favourite fishing-place, Kistnapatam. An old bungalow stood there by a swampy patch between the canal and a wide estuary which, by repute, runs to sixty feet in depth. Occasionally a little fever occurred there, but it was nothing to the malaria which devastated the coast south of the backwater. That region used to be healthy enough down to the jungle-covered island of Srīharikōta, the traditional habitat of Yānādis and malaria. The extension of the disease northward is perhaps to be attributed to the formation of casuarina plantations along the shore and to the consequent spread of mosquitoes which at Duggarāzupatnam are so virulent that the people, according to report, secure their night's rest by burying themselves at the worst season in the sea-sand, leaving the face only uncovered. Not far from that spot, near Armeghon, where the English made their first settlement in 1625, a burning steamer came ashore and for two months it lay there on fire. The report of the occurrence sent to me by the Station-house Officer stated that there was "great burning and various sorts of smells."

At Kistnapatam occurred the only death from the bite of a sea-snake which came to my personal knowledge. A cooly was unloading a boat in the canal when he was bitten. He started to walk to his home a mile off, but died on the way. Anyone who wants to see these reptiles should go to the shallow lagoon which forms the mouth of the Pennēr. I lay a day or two there in a house-boat, and a pretty sight it was to see the surf springing up in silvery fountains from behind the sandspit which hid the sea. As to the snakes, they were everywhere; festooned along the shore, lying coiled and motionless just below the surface. To enter the water seemed certain death, yet the fishermen dashed in with nets, making, I noticed, an unusual amount of splashing and working in gangs. I asked whether they were not afraid. Yes, but what were they to do? They must live.

Shuttleworth, the doctor, told me that near Port Blair in the Andamans there is an island, known as Snake Island, which at high tide shows only a small patch of broken rock above the surface. He and another went to visit it and, in landing, they managed to damage the boat badly. Consequently from 10 a.m. till after dark the pair were on the islet, for the most part under a blazing sun. They well-nigh died of thirst and were in much alarm over the sea-snakes, which came crawling in great numbers out of the sea on to the rocks. They had no sticks, but killed a score or so with stones and suffered no mishap.

Nellore is quite as prolific of land-snakes as of sea-snakes. The former are indeed extraordinarily abundant, and among them is the Banded Krait, which is not generally supposed, as I understand, to come so far south. As a fact I met with this snake in the south of Madura district, so it clearly occurs throughout the Peninsula. Twice I saw in my garden snakes in conjugation ; in the one case rat-snakes, in the other remarkably fine kraits. Reared up to a third or a half of their length, they swing from side to side in graceful unison and at times interlace their necks and assume the exact position of the serpents on Hermes' wand in a sinuous and charming dance.

Scorpions also swarm, and, out Udayagiri way, there is said to be a particularly dangerous sort. In the school of S., the missionary, a boy was stung by a big black one, became unconscious, and sweated to such an extent that he lay in a sort of puddle. This boy seemingly recovered, but both S. and a Tahsildar testified to cases of adults dying from scorpion-sting, and a native gentleman told me that his son had been killed by one. L. saw one of the large black ones seize, sting to death, and carry off a young squirrel. My peons and servants were often stung and used indigenous remedies which seemed to be effective, or were treated with the electric battery which generally, though not always, gave early relief. When the battery was applied to my servant Muniswāmi, and he found that he could not let go of the handles, his terror was ludicrous. He rolled over and over on the ground yelling, "Bub-bub-bubba" and "Ammā, Ammā" (Mamma, Mamma), until we let him free and applied a native drug.

In the matter of heat, the district of Nellore deserves the utmost respect for the business-like way in which it works up the temperature. May is simply appalling. About the first of that month a wild and burning wind arrives from the west, and for weeks, under a sky gray with dust, that blast from the Pit rages and bellows. Yet even this horrible gale seems preferable to the breathless nocturnal intervals of sullen, brooding heat, and it is almost a relief when, with clash of doors and rattle of venetians, the wind sweeps down again on the suffering land.

Some small measure of respite is, indeed, obtainable. There are bungalows scattered along the shore where, at least, it looks cooler and where for a few hours a slight sea-breeze does bring some solace, and there are also two hills of well over 3,000 feet. Of these one, Pentsalakonda, is in the Veligondas. It attains 3,653 feet, and Baillie and I got in two hours to the top, where there is a level patch of grass, some trees and flowers, and a deep pool, but there is no house on this hill and it would be difficult to get tents up.

The other hill is Udayagiri—the Red Mountain. This is a detached summit with a grand scarp of high, ruddy cliffs and a fine, bluff outline. Walls encircle it, ruined walls which cling to cliff-edges and vanish amongst overspreading vegetation. When you have gained the tableland which slopes upward on either hand from the cleft through which creeps the one narrow and erstwhile defended path, you find yourself surrounded by tumbled boulders and masses of crumbling masonry. The fortress, or

Drūg, was of much importance in the days of the old dynasties and must have possessed great strength. Various inscriptions cut on stone are to be found on the hill. One, of the seventeenth century, records the laying-out of a garden which was the "Paradise of Paradises," and over which a wandering angel paused to murmur, "How beautiful!" Another refers to some ancient battle on the hill, and a third recites the claims to admiration of a follower of the Prophet who burnt "the sweepings of idolatry," destroyed the worshippers of idols, and, by his capture of the stronghold, "filled the world as it were with jessamine flowers." It was this devoted servant of the All-Merciful who built the largest mosque in Udayagiri.

The village below the hill has since ancient days been supplied with water from it by a covered conduit, but the supply is inadequate and, in times of drought, the people wait for hours to get a potful from the bottom of wells which in wet weather hold forty or fifty feet of water.

On the hill the only inhabitants consist of a small community of Muttrāchas, of whose means of livelihood the gathering of honey is one. The bees' nest being on the face of a cliff, a man is let down by a rope to which is attached a stout stem of some sort with portions of the branches left on it to serve as steps. This compensates for any small excess or deficiency in the length of rope paid out. The climber carries a long pole with a bunch of grass at the end and a bamboo to which a leather bag is attached; a bundle of straw is tied to the stem. The bunch and bundle being lighted, the former is thrust under the nest, and the bees, which swarm out boisterously, are prevented from attacking the man by the smoke from the bundle. Then the comb is scooped off with the bag.

Occasionally a panther appears on the hill. The watchman of the forest bungalow bore the claw-marks of one. He wounded the animal, followed it boldly into a cave, and was lucky to escape as he did. There are said to be lots of pythons, and ants swarm to such an extent that at the mission bungalow, in one night, they killed, and for the most part devoured, sixteen chickens.

A Eurasian Forest Ranger, who visited me on the hill, entertained me with some stories. He claimed to have witnessed a fight between a tiger and a sambhur stag. The former came off victorious, but was so badly hurt that for hours it ranged about the scene of conflict roaring. Then came a more remarkable episode. The Ranger, when out with some others, met two men who declared that a tiger was on their heels. All the party thereupon took refuge in a hut, before which the baffled pursuer sat down. After keeping up the siege for a while, the tiger hid itself in the neighbourhood, but the besieged were not to be tempted out. Some hours passed and then a cart appeared with some women walking behind it. On one of these the tiger sprang. The narrator's account of the earlier history of that tiger was so improbable as to throw doubt upon the whole story.

I have referred to the inscriptions to be found on Udayagiri. Such, on stone or copper-plates, are common throughout the district and, to the number of more than nine hundred, ranging over eleven centuries, they were copied and translated through the efforts of a Sub-Collector of the district (Mr. Venugōpāl Chetti) and myself. Most of them are wholly uninteresting ; grants of land for the support of temples and so on, sometimes ending with rather comically indecent curses upon those who may violate the grant. Some are queer spells to ward off disease from men or cattle. A few are in an unknown script. Most are in Sanskrit, Telugu, or Tamil, but other languages are represented. There is pathos in this Arabic one, which seems to be addressed to some woman in the writer's family : "Continuous severe illness which wears out the sufferer. Compared with such illness Death is of no account. Indeed, O Ayesha, such illness makes life bitter. Death is near to furnish the proof [*i.e.* that it is preferable to life]."

The only other inscription which I will quote is this one : "Never have I desire for the enjoyment of celestial maidens. I seek not the glory of attaining the illustrious abode of Brahmā and the other Gods, nor does my mind dwell upon the eight forms of wealth. But I pray, O Hara, for very deep faith in the lotus of Thy feet." Not far, this man, from the Kingdom of God.

There is not in Nellore a single building of any structural merit, and it may be said generally that the Telugus show little trace of the architectural capacity of the Tamils. The most noticeable pagoda is that of Ranganāyakaluswāmi at Nellore. There, at the Rathotsava festival, when the huge temple-car is dragged, creaking and groaning, along the streets, people may be seen casting down pumpkins to be squashed under the wheels, possibly an attenuated survival of the old-time horrors of the Car of Juggernaut, and perchance there will be observed a devotee standing steady on his head with legs apart and chanting, "Harē, Harē."

Opposite the temple at Sangam, where the Pennēr is dammed to form the rice-growing delta, there is a very large obelisk. Unhappily it has been broken into three pieces, but the portion still upright may be thirty feet high. It is decorated with scrollwork of a stereotyped but remarkably pleasing pattern. Tanks there are in plenty, ranging downwards from the vast Kaligiri Reservoir with a waterspread of twenty-five square miles. One lay just behind my house. It was generally thronged with waders and swimmers and always swept by the long wings of the graceful, circling terns. On its shore I saw one morning a pariah-dog which had adopted me as its patron gnawing the corpse of a woman. The servants prophesied that the dog would go mad after its horrible meal, but it did not do so. The woman was supposed to have committed suicide, for which this land of tanks and wells affords women every facility. A remarkable case of suicide by drowning occurred at Coonoor. Three Badaga women swathed themselves and two babies in a winding-sheet formed of their united cloths and flung themselves into the drinking-water reservoir. All the five were drowned, and I never heard the reason for the act. I recall, too, the case of an old man in Nellore (he was said to be eighty or ninety years of age) who, weary of the ceaseless come and go of days flavoured only with bitter poverty, sought to end his troubles by the horrible device of chopping off his genital organs with an axe. Strange to say, he recovered from his frightful injuries and lived for a year or so longer. Arrangements were made that, during that remnant of life, he should not want for food at all events. Only too many of my European acquaintances in India have died by their own hands, and I do not remember a single case where a motive could be assigned ; always the deed was done in response to the muttered promptings of that *nescio quid doloris* which lurks in our souls.

Our small society at Nellore included a *corps d'élite* of alcoholists and a group of Baptist missionaries.

On one, and only one, occasion there were signs of a *rapprochement* between these two bodies. It happened, says tradition, in the days when the district was under Guest, Guest whom everybody loved. At the Collector's Christmas dinner Duffy, the little missionary, was present. As the champagne circulated, Duffy grew animated. He slapped his host on the back, called him "old fellow," and laughed heartily. Later he grew very grave and silent and seemed sunk in meditation as he slipped lower and lower in his chair. The ladies left. The cup went round. When the men rose in their turn, Duffy was on the floor, but his absence was not noticed until later on, in the drawing-room, Mrs. Duffy raised the question of his whereabouts. Some idle speculation on the subject followed. Suddenly the lady gave a piercing scream and pointed. At the door stood Duffy. His mournful face was mostly occupied with mud and green slime. His clothes were similarly stained and clung closely to him. From his hair drops oozed, and with it were mingled waterweeds. What had happened was never clearly explained, but it seems that, finding himself under the table, Duffy lay for a space wondering and then rose and strayed in bewilderment into the garden, where he fell into one of the sunk cisterns used for watering the plants.

The arrival of Baillie, a newly-landed Civilian, for the purpose of undergoing training provided me with companionship in camp which partially reconciled me to the tactless rapidity with which he outdistanced me in shooting and in Telugu. I appointed him to be my Taster, as at times I liked to make trial of strange foods, and I was convinced of the utility of the post when he started hungrily upon a dogfish as to the edibility of which I felt curious. This happened at Rāmayyapatnam where of yore a Sub-

Collector was stationed. In the compound of his house, which has passed to the missionaries, there stands a large tomb built apparently over a favourite dog. The inscription on it is, "To Cæto. Cur non? 1827."

At Isakapalli both Baillie and I had visions of sudden death. The former swam out some way from the beach, then turned and came hastily back, his face working strangely. Arrived, he spoke no word, but sped homewards stark naked. Fortunately our temporary abode was not far off. When I in turn got there, I found that he was suffering from symptoms more comical than alarming, and we came to the conclusion that he had been stung by a jelly-fish and not bitten by a sea-snake as he at first supposed. As for my own experience, it happened when Baillie and I were out on catamarans, which consist of four or five curved and shaped logs lashed together—the safest craft in the world. We resolved to swim back through the surf. My strength proved inadequate, and I was about to surrender to the soft allurement of repose which steeped my every sense when instinct prompted two more strokes and I was helped on to a catamaran. I felt ill for some days afterwards.

The District of Nellore contains the huge Zamindāri of Venkatagiri, which covers some 2,000 square miles and is owned by a family which for centuries has held high position in the south. When I first came in sight, on topping a rise, of the Raja's capital, I reined in, as I remember, in surprise at the scene. I do not know why it was, but for some time previously I had been, as it were, obsessed by visions of a wonderful country wherein white palaces showed against green hills. These came to me so often in a half-waking state that, at times, I almost doubted whether I was moving in that world or in this. What I saw, looking at Venkatagiri from a distance, was much the scene of my dreams, but the illusion faded as I drew nearer and as the marble façades degenerated into the white fronts of the large but commonplace houses of the Raja and his brothers.

In the Venkatagiri Darbar-hall there is a wooden throne covered with thin gold plates or, where renewal has been necessary, with plates of gilded silver. This seat and a big emerald are said to have been presented to the Zamindāri family by one of the kings of Vijayanagar and to have seen many vicissitudes. An unusual thing to be seen at Venkatagiri is a mosque built by a Hindu, to wit, the great-grandfather of the Raja of my time; a little pressure on the part of the Muhammadan ruler may be surmised. There are, of course, temples in the town, and my visit to one of them served as a reason for squeezing money out of the Raja for the performance of ceremonies of purification. I found in the town, in addition, a must elephant moving restlessly in chains which it had worn for three months. The recollection calls before me another Zamindar, who may be referred to as Z. This gentleman borrowed a temple elephant to grace his Dasserah procession. In the first place, it had to be towed behind a steamer across a mile or so of water and well-nigh perished in the process. Then, when it had recovered, the Sub-Divisional Magistrate forbade its use in procession on the ground that it was must and was reported to have injured two people. Against this order Z. appealed to the District Magistrate, asking that officer to consider whether he was the sort of man who would have anything to do with a must elephant. As the District Magistrate was able conscientiously to answer this question in the negative, he cancelled the prohibition, but did so conditionally upon Z. riding the animal himself in the procession. Apparently this was not the plan which Z. had in view, and he fell to regretting his ill-advised appeal. However, his reputation being now involved, he bravely determined to face the risk. Meanwhile precautionary measures would not be out of place. The elephant was continuously and heavily dosed with opium so that, indeed, it could hardly keep its feet when, on the ceremonial day, the portly frame of the unhappy nobleman was hoisted on to it. The procession passed off without a hitch, but the Sub-Divisional Magistrate's order found justification when, a few weeks later, the animal made its condition manifest by killing its mahout.

From Venkatagiri I went on with Baillie to Pālemkōta, where the Raja had two small shooting-boxes. In spite of the woodmanship of our Yānādis, no sport was got. Tigers now and again visit this locality and are sometimes shot from behind low screens of leaves run up alongside the tracks down which the beaters will drive them. It sounds a very dangerous method, but it is asserted to be quite the reverse, the tiger, on receiving the ball, either dropping or bounding straight forward on its path without a glance to right or left.

Over Pālemkōta tower to a height of 3,200 feet the red cliffs of Venkatagiri Drūg. It took a couple of hours to reach the top. The last thousand feet or so consist of a monstrous shaft of rock which is scaled by steps and a winding path. There are traces of works of defence: two gateways, some rough walls, and, on the summit which is only about two hundred yards across, a few intact buildings, and even fragments of a cannon. The hill used to serve as a place of refuge for the Chiefs of Venkatagiri when oppressed by more powerful potentates.

Not far from this neighbourhood and near Rāpur

I spent a good deal cf time and toil in fruitless attempts to gain trophies. On one occasion my efforts extended over four days and I was accompanied by Yānādi shikāris and fifty beaters. The first day, from behind a screen of leaves, I heard a panther go off roaring to one side and a sambhur crashing to the other. Pigs also approached, but nothing bigger than a mongoose came into view, so four hours of trudging were wasted. The next day we drew blank. On its successor a she-bear with cubs was started, and the beaters amused me afterwards with a spirited imitation of the "gug-gug-gug" of the mother as she made for one of the party and the shrill cries of that person as he mounted a tree. But I saw nothing of the animal, and the fourth day also was a blank. On another occasion Baillie and I beat a fine ravine after a long walk. It contained three bears, a panther, and a sambhur, but they did not show up. Then, gasping and sweating, we climbed some 800 feet to another glen. A scratch of a claw on a rock, a whispered "puli," and I turned in time to see the fat tail of a tiger flourish as it disappeared over a rock. A great disappointment, for we failed to get another glimpse of the animal.

The then Raja of Venkatagiri told me that there used to be bison in the southern part of his estate and that his father killed the last of them, thus destroying for ever a most interesting portion of the fauna of Nellore. The Raja himself did a good deal of shooting at one time, and, after my time in the district, fell a victim to a stray bullet during a beat. I remember only one similar fatal accident in a beat, but I have heard of a man killing his companion when sitting over a tie. In that case the other man left his tree, apparently in order to see whether the bait was secure, and in the darkness was mistaken by his friend for the animal they were after. Incidentally I may give here an example of the boldness of the panther. Baillie was sitting on the ground by a kill awaiting one of these animals. Some wild-dogs appeared, and he shot one and laid it behind him. Soon afterwards a slight sound in the rear made him turn just in time to get a glimpse of the panther making off with the dead dog.

The people of Nellore are firmly convinced that the tiger and panther breed together and produce an animal which they call "ibbandigādu" (the troublesome one), a term applied in some places to the panther itself. A Tahsildar told me that he had seen skins of this animal and that they bore both spots and stripes, but my belief is that any unusually big panther may get credit for such mixed parentage.

It was another of my Tahsildars who was regarded as an expert on indigenous medicine. He supplied me with a remedy for the bite of a mad dog, which is to sit for some time alongside a Yerakkam plant (*Calotropis gigantea*). To secure general health, he advocated breathing on alternate days through alternate nostrils, but how he compassed this I do not know. Doubtless quite as efficacious was a prescription for whooping-cough which was supplied by an ayah: "Give the child black-monkey's mutton or, if that cannot be got, worms chopped up and fried in ghee." From a book called "Thirty Minor Upanishads" I learnt that graying of the hair can be staved off by standing on the head for some time every day for three months.

There was a schoolmaster, I remember, who put in an application for a licence to carry a gun in order to shoot flying-foxes to be eaten as a cure for short-sight. This application being rejected, he put in another in which he stated that he needed a gun to kill "jackals, pigs, hyænas, and other herbivorous insects."

As another instance of the strange notions prevalent on the subject of disease, I may refer to a question put to the Government by a member of the local Legislative Council. Remarking that there was a burning ground close to the Madura Bridge railway station, he asked whether the Government would order the removal of that station to another site for the reason that the reek of burning grounds is prejudicial to the health of persons suffering from the bites of mad dogs. The Government declined to take any action, not being convinced that any considerable proportion of the travelling public is affected with hydrophobia in an incipient form. Conceivably the percentage may be high in the case of the stationary population of Nellore, for outbreaks of rabies are remarkably frequent there. The unhappy case of S. of the Police did not, however, occur in that district. He had wounded a tiger or panther near his abode, and at night his servants came to tell him that some animal with glaring eyes was in the elephant shed. They thought that it might be the wounded beast, and S. went out to see. When he got to the shed, a mad wild-dog rushed out and bit him. He went to the Pasteur Institute at Coonoor, but succumbed, dying peacefully, however. Just outside the Nellore district, not far from Tada, where people quarry a beautiful, pinkish building-stone and whence they take boat to cross the large, shallow lagoon known as Pulicat Lake for the overgrown island of Srīharikota, there is a place which abounds in panthers. There Hatfield had a narrow escape while following a wounded one. The shikāri told him that the beast was lying in a clump of bushes. He peered into it, but, in that diapering of shine and shadow, could see nothing. A spot of white flicked across. He knew that it was the animal's tail, yet, sharp as his eyes are and gaze as he would, he still could not distinguish the body. Again the warning signal flew, and still he peered in vain. Then up against his face was a sudden vision of teeth and flashing eyes. He leapt to the rear and fell on his back over a root. The panther's spring carried it to his feet, and there it stayed a space. Hatfield could not help laughing at the absurdity of their postures, but the scene was broken into by a Yānādi who bravely sprang between, and with shouts and flourishings of his bill-hook scared the animal away.

I have loitered about the southern part of the district quite long enough and will now move elsewhither, village after village welcoming my arrival with a band, a bevy of dancing-girls, or even a *posse* of capering, somersaulting Mādigas. My carts labouring across the fields at the rate of ten miles in nine hours, I reached Tsundi, the headquarters of a small Zamindāri, which perhaps represents in shrunken form the domains of the old Reddi dynasty. The place contains the outline of a fort, two or three small temples, and a fine monolithic obelisk about forty feet high. The estate had been neglected in the usual way and, after some negotiations, the Court of Wards stepped in and appointed a Manager. Apparently the change created some ill-feeling, for soon afterwards I received from the Manager the following telegram: "Attempted murdering Revenue Inspector. Fourth night hundreds besieged camp. Deadly stones rained 9 to 2. Very narrow escape. Great consternation in camp. Frenzy throughout estate. Possession very dangerous. Retreating for safety till sufficiently reinforced." The Superintendent of Police went to the spot and found that there had been a trifling *fracas*. No doubt he made his opinion of the Manager sufficiently clear to that functionary.

This northern part of the district was then under the control of a Sub-Collector named Aylwin, who presented a rather unusual combination of literary proclivities with a positive zest for danger. It fell to his lot once to quell a serious riot, and, in describing the occurrence to me, he mentioned that he had always envied the experiences of those who knew India during the Mutiny. Fate in the end did not deny him a full share of that which he coveted, for a few years later he was murdered by one of the so-called Nationalist party. Like several other victims of political fanaticism, he went out of his way to be cordial to, and familiar with, the Indian community.

In company with Aylwin I toured the Sub-Division, which included those detached portions of the Venkatagiri estate which are known as Pōdili and Darsi. The latter is one of the dreariest parts of the world, but the humble village from which it takes its name showed unexpected consciousness of co-partnership in empire when it sent through me a present to the King, which doubtless reached him in due course. The gift consisted of a talisman which, after being consecrated and worshipped in the temple, was enclosed in a rough gold locket. Along with this was sent an account in English of the ceremony attendant upon consecration. The procession of villagers was said to have been of "indescribable grandeur," and the speeches, reported in full, were punctuated with such remarks as "Thanks with loud shouts," "No, no, shouts of joy."

Pōdili is not so unattractive an area as Darsi, for it includes a group of hills which rise above 2,000 feet, and the general monotonous flatness is further relieved here and there by high knife-blades produced by the weathering of rocky outcrops into vertical slabs. We made several ascents of the Pōdili Hills after bears, of which some were sighted but none was got. There is a village called Pōdili close to the hills, and the principal industry of that place seemed to be the stoning of unpopular characters. At one time this business centred round a Baptist missionary, but, when I visited the place, the Deputy Tahsildar was engaging attention, and was stoned nightly by the serious-minded.

I returned to Nellore to encounter a small disturbance between Hindus and Muhammadans in the town and trouble in my own house. There was a quarrel between the servants, and one of them found on the premises two small metal plates figured as spells. There fell upon the household great fear in the midst of which I moved into camp again. Then the maty died, crying out that he was the victim of evil practices which would have come to naught had the "Doragāru" only remained in the place. The cause of his death was never clearly ascertained.

At Nellore I witnessed the Firewalking Ceremony. In this exhibition there was dug a trench about eight yards long by three broad. This was filled with glowing embers, the heat from which was so great as to turn me somewhat faint. At the end of the trench was a ditch full of water. The performers were Pallikāpus from North Arcot. They were smeared with saffron and hung with garlands, and one wore on his head a huge structure made apparently of paper. It was said that, before the show began, a sheep had been killed and its blood had been sprinkled in the trench. The performers walked quickly, barefoot, over the embers, and jumped into the ditch when they got to the end of the trench. They repeated the performance twice or thrice, some walking and others running. None apparently was hurt in any way. It was stated that the men had previously soaked their feet in water for a long while, and, of course, people who habitually go barefoot can bear a degree of heat which would be intolerable to our soles.

When His Excellency the Governor came to stay with me at this time, I noticed with regret that all the native inhabitants who came to pay him their respects and who habitually wore a loin-cloth and a strip of muslin over one shoulder and, so attired, looked respectable and amply dressed, had thought it proper to indue shabby "Europe" coats, which, with the collars turned up, gave them a dilapidated look. The unsuitability of our ugly European costume for the tropics is so obvious that it is somewhat surprising that it has not been materially modified, but I remember only one reformer in this direction. He presided in Court in a cotton vest with a towel round his waist, but had the usual fate of reformers.

A visit by a Governor to a Collector has been defined as a sentence of three days' rigorous imprisonment and a fine of a thousand rupees. I was in fear lest my sentence should be enhanced, for on the last night there fell a deluge of rain equalling, or exceeding, anything I have known on the West Coast. In twelve hours ten inches of water descended. I lay quaking, in anticipation of the flooding of the railway line, and it was in fact breached, but an hour after the Governor had left. His last view of Nellore embraced a heavy and complicated fall on the part of a mounted Inspector. His whole visit had been brightened by such impromptu entertainments on the part of the mounted Police. They culminated in a grand acrobatic display at the Judge's exhibition of fireworks.

At that period breaches of the East Coast railway line were a common sequence of a heavy downpour. I remember a train pulling up at a place where, owing to damage to the permanent way, water was rushing under the rails. The passengers were carried across in trolleys, but there was a Frenchman who preferred to do the bit on foot. On the other side we were joined by this gentleman, who was much excited and pouring with sweat. A compatriot remarked that he seemed to feel the heat a good deal. I liked the frank answer : "Ce n'est pas la chaleur ; c'est la peur." A man I knew was in a train which was held up by breaches in front and behind. The whole country was under water, and the wretched passengers, who could get very little food, were kept there for four days. Very violent rain is sometimes presaged by the appearance of enormous rays of pink light which spring from the setting sun.

I had many guests besides the Governor, among them Humby and MacIntyre. Both were gifted conversationally ; the former with a prodigious, dull loquacity ; the other with a delightful capacity for telling facetious stories. Humby was a man of exemplary piety, and very kind and generous to boot. He also ran to fat. A man said of him, with extraordinary aptness, "I have often heard of the milk of human kindness but I never came across the cow before."

MacIntyre had just been to visit the Kolar goldmines, round which he had been shown by a Cornish miner, who gave him to understand that, albeit deficient in the grammatical and literary niceties of Tamil, he possessed a fluent, conversational knowledge of that tongue. The only examples of his Tamil which MacIntyre heard were these : "'Ere, *pēsādē*, there's good fellows. Why I can 'ardly 'ear myself speak," and "Now then, *sīkkiram* with that *lānthar*. I shall be breaking my shins over something before long." These idiomatic Tamil sentences remind one of Rudyard Kipling's Hindustani phrase-book for soldiers: "*Jaldi* with those fried kidneys or I'll *garram* your *pīchche*," and so on. MacIntyre also recounted to me the particulars of an experience which had recently fallen to the lot of Fenton, the President of the Madras Corporation. He and Fraser the lawyer had been spending a quiet evening at the Club. They left it about 2 a.m. in Fenton's dogcart. Fraser was in a state of deep depression, but Fenton was exceedingly cheerful and chatty, and, as he drove, he talked blithely to Fraser, who responded in monosyllables. Fraser was not, however, so sunk in melancholy as to be quite oblivious to what was going on. He observed that the pony was travelling very fast, and, conceiving that Fenton might have dropped the reins accidentally, he began feeling about for them. In doing so, he chanced to overbalance and fell out onto the road. The pony continued to gallop and Fenton continued to talk, but, missing after a time Fraser's customary monosyllables, the President glanced towards his companion's seat and noticed with surprise that it was empty. Still he felt satisfied that Fraser was somewhere about and that it was merely a matter of careful search to find him. Therefore he dropped the reins, and felt round for the missing man. Giving up the quest after a time, he bethought him of the reins and started looking for them. He lit on the crupper instead and got hold of it with both hands, under the impression that he was holding the reins. Owing to this unfortunate mistake, which was due to the darkness of the night, when Fenton attempted to pull the pony up sharply, he was lifted out of the vehicle and suffered a heavy and painful fall. A few yards farther up the road the pony ran into something, and the empty dogcart was smashed to pieces, so that it is permissible to regard the accidents which had befallen the two men as providentially designed for the saving of their lives.

The last episode which I shall refer to as affecting Nellore presents some pleasingly Oriental *traits*. Some two years or so previously a serious railway accident had happened in Cuddapah. Amongst the victims was a Parsi jeweller from Bombay, who had in his possession a quantity of valuables, which disappeared from the scene of the disaster and were never traced. One day a European mica-miner of the Nellore district came to the Superintendent of Police with information that a gang of Kattiras (a tribe of wandering thieves) were trying to dispose in his neighbourhood of various valuable things. It occurred to the Superintendent that this might be a party which had looted the wrecked train, and, the case being important, he procured from Madras two detectives, of whom one was sent to the mica-miner to pose as his butler, while the other was told off, disguised as a beggar, to fraternize with the Kattiras. The latter played his part so well that the suspects gave him one of their women to serve as a wife. For awhile nothing happened. Then it befell that the constable who, as a matter of form, had been attached to the gang to keep ostensible watch upon its movements and who daily collected a gratuity for himself from each of the Kattiras and from the beggar whose identity was unknown to him—it befell, I say, that this constable called upon the beggar to make to him a second payment of four annas on one and the same day. The beggar refused to comply with this novel and unjust demand, whereupon the constable, moved with indignation, called together the village magistrate and other elders and invited them to declare the beggar to be a rogue, vagabond, and general *badmāsh*. This having been duly done, the beggar was formally arrested by the constable and stowed in the lock-up attached to the police-station at Y. At the moment the Superintendent, satisfied with the information which had so far reached him, was engaged in quietly collecting his reserve and in perfecting arrangements for a great midnight drive which was to sweep all the Kattiras and their belongings into his net. The beggar's stay in the lock-up had exceeded by four times the legal limit when a constable entered the Y. police-station and, in conversation with the head constable, remarked that the Superintendent was getting the reserve together. The head constable was shrewd. "That means," he said, "that he is going to raid the Kattiras"; and he added, foreseeing much advantage to himself, "we must hasten to warn them." So saying, the head constable departed on his charitable mission. That night the drive took place but the birds had flown. Then the beggar-detective made revelation of himself, and the head constable was haled before the Magistrate.

Whilst serving in this district I made a tour of some of the principal places in Northern India. I saw, of course, the Tāj-mahāl, and so realized that sense of deep and abiding sorrow which in some inexplicable way it leaves on the mind and which no picture of it indicates in the smallest degree. Why the tomb of Itiwād-ud-doulah of similar design, though on a much smaller scale, should produce an effect in such sharp contrast, an effect of gay and charming coquetry, I am at a loss to understand. The supreme beauty of Shah Jehān's edifice impressed me more than it did an American tourist whom B. met. Coming across that gentleman at the close of his visit to

Northern India, B. asked him the usual question whether he had seen the Tāj. The American hesitated a moment and then answered: "The Tajj—well, I can't say that I exactly recall it; but I saw it, you bet I saw it; I had a very good guide."

Of the other glories of the north it is not my purpose to speak.

Lucknow's crowd of mean palaces and Cawnpore, still instinct with tragedy, may be passed by.

Benares I recall only to mention the strange, narrow alleys where they sell among other things, smooth, testiculate stones for application to the persons of women in want of children, and the enclosure which forms the burial-place of "brave men who died" (in 1781) "in the execution of their duty."

Fattehpur-Sikri I visited in company with two Americans, father and son. On the way we came on a fine bull which the young man wanted to photograph. So the carriage was stopped and he got out, set up his camera in the road, and disappeared under the cloth. Then the bull charged, and the agility of the young man's subsequent movements caused lively satisfaction to me and his unnatural parent.

Imperial Delhi itself shall supply but one reminiscence, the well-known and touching epitaph: "Let no rich coverlet adorn my grave. This grass is the best covering for the tomb of the poor in spirit, the humble, the transitory Jahānārā, the disciple of the holy men of Chist, the daughter of the Emperor Shah Jehān." Of lowlier parentage was the woman who lies in the little cemetery at Nellore. Her tombstone bears the name "Mary Dalrymple," nothing more, and to whom this musical assemblage of syllables belonged I do not know.

CHAPTER XII

TRICHINOPOLY

IT is fortunate that among the Tamils the profound religiousness of India has taken concrete form in temples, because, in whatever way these may offend against the canons of Art, they are yet, by virtue of size, originality, and luxuriance of detail, among the prominent architectural products of the world. The general type of structure, reproduced indeed with monotonous frequency, has been described already. Its main characteristic may be said to be the principle of diminishing effect, an inevitable result of the growth of these great edifices by successive accretions to ancient shrines of small size. There are, however, instances of divergence from the ordinary plan. In the Tanjore temple, for example, the vimāna (the structure surmounting the shrine) is much higher than the gopurams over the gateways of approach, while, in the little-known but more boldly wrought temple at Gangaikandapuram in the Trichinopoly district, the vimāna is the only conspicuous feature. In this latter district there are pagodas of a third sort ; high, solid, stone buildings, reared on hillocks and dominating the country like baronial castles. This resemblance has not always stopped at outward seeming, for sharp fights for the possession of some of them took place in the days of English and French warfare. Of such struggles the best known is that which filled with spirts of flame and cries and sudden tramplings a strange night of surprises, the night when Clive, faint from loss of blood, reeled against a door-jamb of the Samayavaram temple and so escaped the bullet which killed the soldier alongside him.

Conspicuous among the hill-sanctuaries of the district is that which crowns the great rock at Trichinopoly. The approach thereto is unusual, for the long flight of steps leading up the rock is roofed over to form a tunnel which is broken here and there by openings to admit light and by recesses containing shrines. At dawn the summit hovers as a floating island above the misty ground, and the sun, when it outlines sharply the high and frowning walls of the temple and the bold crag on which it stands, strikes from the gilded pinnacle a flash which is visible a score of miles away. The rock contains some cave-temples of about the seventh century, and at its foot lies a handsome, square, stone tank surrounded by an irregular mass of buildings comprising the old main-guard, shops, houses, and colleges. That bit of the town makes an admirable picture, but, for the most part, the city is ill-built and ill-kept. It is matter for surprise that Trichinopoly should be so poorly provided with relics of the past, for it was long the headquarters of the great Chōla dynasty. No material indications of that fact remain, and, although there are some traces of the later Nāyakkar line of Madura, they have no particular merit, while of the subsequent period of warfare no notable memorial exists except Dalton's Battery and the Main Guard gate. One other edifice may be mentioned for the sake of the inscription in Tamil and Hindustani which it bears. That building is the old Court-house, and the inscription runs as follows :—

"Whereas the men of this country foolishly deceived persons in various ways and ruined them and with a view to prevent the commission of similar misdeeds in the future and to administer justice, be it known that this Court-house was, under the orders of the Honourable English Company, built on the 1st day of July 1804 by Walter Colfield Lennan in the style which seemed good to his mind."

As to the condition of Mr. Lennan's mind from the artistic point of view people who see the building will draw their own conclusions.

Treasure-troves, memorials of troublous times, are frequent in India. In Nellore there was in my time a find of Roman *aurei* at Tangatūr. It was believed that all the coins were melted down by the finder except one, which was in excellent preservation and bore on one side a well-executed head of Hadrianus Augustus and on the other a clumsy figure of a mounted spearman with "C. os III." Again, at Kodūr in that district a man dug up a potful of gold coins valued at R.50,000. He did not report the matter, but it reached the ears of the Tahsildar, who declared the find forfeit and started further excavations. As a result, several copper pots covered with a sort of plaster and containing gold coins valued at R.100,000 were unearthed by the Tahsildar, who claimed the finder's legal share. The claim was rejected and perhaps was not tenable, but the Government acted meanly in allowing to the Tahsildar only a thousand rupees out of this large windfall to the exchequer.

While I was at Trichinopoly there were several discoveries of buried bronze idols (one a work of great merit) and other things. The best batch of images was found in a rather curious way. A certain native Christian, it appears, made profession of his ability to find hidden treasure in a specified place. Ramsay and Babbage of the Railway and others formed a syndicate to find funds for digging under the Christian's directions, and one day Babbage, with a broad smile on his face, brought into my office several peculiar, old metal pots containing 500 small gold coins and, also, a number of gold ornaments, some of which were of tasteful design and delicate finish. Later on the bronze figures were dug up at the same place, which was the site of an old brick building, by tradition a palace.

There is at Trichinopoly a rock called Chōlampārai which bears an inscription relative to the endowment of a temple with certain lands. An old mistranslation represented it as stating that a number of chests of treasure lay buried under the rock. A Collector of past days who found nothing remarkable in such public advertisement of the concealment of wealth induced an equally simple Government to undertake excavations which were, of course, fruitless. Afterwards the quest was undertaken again, this time by a syndicate composed of Babbage and others, who secured, on payment of a fee, a permit to dig under the rock. Undaunted by initial ill-success, they applied to me for an extension of the permit and, although informed of the true meaning of the epigraph, pressed their request. In the end the members of the syndicate were the richer by the lid of a pot and a modern copper coin. However, they were more fortunate than some treasure-seekers in Nellore, who set to work to dig under a big inscribed stone, with the result that it fell and killed one of the excavators.

A treasure-hunter of another sort was a Brahman, who devoted a remarkable talent for climbing to collecting the apical ornaments of temples, such being sometimes covered with gold more or less alloyed.

Among other trophies he secured by a perilous climb the "stūpi" of the Rock Temple at Trichinopoly. He was captured after this exploit, and amused himself by telling the police that the ornament was in the river. They groped and dived there for hours before he confessed to the real hiding-place, which was the adjacent tank.

If I remember rightly, my district covered between three and four thousand square miles. It has since been somewhat enlarged, but I speak of it as it then existed. Physical features of interest are scarce, but a range called Pachaimalai rises to over 3,000 feet in the north and, southward, the district ends against steep hills, for the most part bare of trees save that here and there the flat-crowned "umbrella trees" project like shelves from their sides. Between these bounds lies a flat tract bisected by the sacred river Kāvēri, which, a little above Trichinopoly town, throws off a great branch, the Coleroon. The main river loses itself in the irrigation channels of Tanjore, into which it is diverted by a dam known as the Grand Anikat. This work dates back to the Chōla kings, but in its present form is modern, and the great barrier makes a fine show of masonry.

The colossal humps and cones of hard, crystalline rock which form so conspicuous a part of Southern Indian scenery are not wanting in Trichinopoly, and away to the west is a mountain-mass called Talaimalai, which culminates in a great dorsal fin of gray stone. On the highest spine of the fin stands a small, mean temple which is said to have been struck by lightning more than once. I found the summit a pleasant spot, although there is nothing to be seen there except a clump of fruit trees, a few acres of grass and hill-dates, abundance of sunshine, and, finally, the temple which, by reason of its defiant position, has something of the charm attaching to fairy-tale pictures of Enchanted Castles.

Of temple-crested hills I had, however, most reason to remember the Perumālkōvil near Turaiyūr. They told me that a thousand steps led to this fane, and I did not believe them. By the time I gained the pagoda, which proved after all to be but a commonplace thing, I had counted 1576 steep, high, glassy steps, and it was an afternoon of March. To descend in safety it was necessary to take the boots off. It may safely be asserted that this is the longest staircase in the world. I certainly felt it to be so.

This hill-pagoda is not far from the Pachaimalai Hills, which bear pretty good forest on their flanks. The ridge-and-dale tableland would grow fine timber, but it is mostly under cultivation. These hills used to be much overpopulated with devils. To abate the nuisance a holy man was imported shortly before my first visit, and by his exertions the number was considerably reduced, but the demon Malaria he was unable to expel.

The southernmost range I ascended at Tōpiswāmimalai, which is some 3,000 feet high. At that point there is some jungle, and it actually contained bison, a fact which I carefully concealed from the sportsmen of Trichinopoly. That any game survived in this patch of woodland was somewhat remarkable, for at the main water-holes were small, cell-like buildings for the use of the Zamindars of Kadavūr, and the Indian sportsman rarely discriminates between male and female, young and old.

The population of the capital of the district runs to six figures, and this mass of humanity included some eighty Europeans, mainly connected with the South Indian Railway. Amongst our military officers was a subaltern named Crowe. One morning the body of this unfortunate young man was found floating in a well in a compound. The head was injured and, of course, rumours of foul play got about. A local amateur detective even took me to see a footmark, alleged to be Crowe's, alongside the print of a bare foot, presumed to be the murderer's. But there was no sufficient reason to doubt that Crowe, wandering for some reason at night into the compound, had stumbled over the low curb of the well and damaged his head in falling. I was at the funeral. The coffin was on a hand-truck, covered with a dirty Union Jack and a tawdry purple pall. Round the grave swarmed a crowd of dog-boys, coolies, and beggars. Eurasians in shabby, ill-made clothes, and Europeans, not much better clad and wearing straw hats or topis of various sorts, completed the attendance. The regiment furnished a discordant band. Not a blade of grass on the iron-bound earth. A melancholy sight. The church by which Crowe is buried contains a tablet in honour of another young man, one Benjamin Horne, who died in 1819. His epitaph closes on a tender note : " This marble was erected by a few friends who knew and loved him."

Concerning our Civil functionaries there is little to say. After I left, one of them was dismissed for corruption, and his was well-nigh the only case of corruption on the part of a European official which occurred in my time. The more to their honour, for many were very inadequately paid. One of our Judges created some excitement by unauthorizedly closing his Court to business. He had been temporarily invalided, and, owing to some irregularity in the filling up of forms, he got no allowances while on leave. The matter being still unsettled when he returned, the Judge declared that he was not going to do any work until he got his pay and closed the

Court for two or three weeks. This led to his removal from the district. One of his successors was, after I left the place, murdered by a Muhammadan who had a grievance against some one and was dissatisfied because the Magistracy would not take action. He appeared with his complaint before the Judge, who could only refer him back to the Magistrate. Enraged by the Judge's refusal to take action, the man lay in wait for him at the entrance of the Court-house and stabbed him as he passed. The murderer was seized at once but broke free, seized a tulwar from one of his guards and wounded another person with it. He was, however, recaptured and executed.

There was a criminal with whom I had something to do in Trichinopoly who showed a somewhat remarkable pertinacity in carrying out his homicidal plans. He was first arraigned for murdering his father, but, although there was little doubt as to his guilt, the evidence was incomplete. On release he made a furious attack upon his mother who had given evidence against him, but the blow he aimed at her was intercepted by a beam in the roof, and he was seized before he could repeat it. For this outrage he went to jail, and, while there, announced his intention to kill all the witnesses who had deposed against him. These threats led to further punishment, but, as soon as he got free, he made murderous assaults on three persons. I found him in jail again on this account, and directed that the Security sections should be applied immediately on the expiry of his term. What happened to him ultimately I do not know.

When I arrived in the district the Railway section of the European community was being annoyed by some person who nursed animosity against it. A mendacious notice appeared in the *Madras Mail* that Mrs. S. had been prematurely delivered of a son.

This was followed by an announcement of her death, but meanwhile S. had got into communication with the editor and this was suppressed. Then, in response to a fictitious order, Mrs. Poulter, who was immensely fat, received from a Madras chemist a communication expressing regret that no "expecting belts" of the size specified were procurable. Finally, there came out in a native newspaper a report that a certain railway official whose identity was but thinly veiled had, in a transport of amorous passion, bitten a Brahman girl so severely in the breast that she had died. The official aimed at secured an apology from the editor, but, as always, it was the lie which made the deeper impression, and many were convinced that the story was true, and, further, that the District Medical Officer had colluded with the culprit in making away with the corpse. Indeed, for some time afterwards, Brahmans would drop in to see the doctor on various pretexts and fish about for inculpatory admissions.

But, if the Railway officers had their secret foes, they were quite capable of holding their own in the open field. One of them, Black, was a tremendous fighter, and constituted a valuable bodyguard to the Traffic Manager. An engine-driver who treated that officer with disrespect was so handled by Black that a party of his mates came in from the works at Negapatam and waylaid the pugilist. A pitiable troop took the return journey. One they left behind as not being in a condition to travel. Black first stunned him and then chivalrously pitched him down a steep bank to save him from being run over on the road.

Babbage of the Railway has been mentioned already. He was a fat man, but Poulter of the Railway was fatter. Indeed Mr. and Mrs. Poulter, together, scaled 34 stone. Babbage and Poulter, forgathering in London, drove in a hansom to a restaurant and tendered the legal fare. Strange to say the driver was not satisfied; stranger still he did not resort to senseless profanity to express his feelings. What he said was this: "Well, it's my legal fare, but all I can say is that I hope, next time you come here in my cab, you'll send your stomachs on in front by Pickford's van."

There grew up in my time a scandal which for a space tore the European community asunder. It would take too long to tell the story, farcical as were some of the details, of that drama of incriminating telegrams, secret conclaves and missives, plans of abduction, and even disguises. In the end the law pronounced the lady to be innocent. She had a way with her, and one of her admirers besought that, in the event of her securing freedom by divorce, she would give him "the second refusal" of her hand, it being assumed, of course, that the expected co-respondent would have the first option. Surely this is a very unusual form of proposal.

There is held every year at Trichinopoly a festival which is highly popular and barbarous. It is called the Blood-drinking ceremony, and the principal performer was an old man, to outward seeming respectable. Black kids were slain by hundreds, and from each victim the venerable vampire drank a drop or two of blood. This feat accomplished, he was raised aloft and borne in triumph by blood-besmeared enthusiasts through a dense crowd of people flinging up their hands to receive the gift of flowers from the garlands which he wore. The ceremony is accompanied by the discordant sounds produced by slender, brass trumpets of such length (over nine feet sometimes) that they are upheld on sticks when blown.

At that period it was still the custom, and it may be so now, for Europeans living at Trichinopoly to arrange that one at least of their servants should be of the Kallan or Thief caste. It was the general belief that, failing such arrangement, burglary was inevitable. Outside headquarters the ryots groaned under a system of blackmail known as Duppukūli, which is organized theft of cattle followed by restitution on payment. The police and magistracy toiled in vain to suppress this form of brigandage by binding over, or imprisoning for failure to procure sureties, those whose crimes or tactlessness towards the police or village bigwigs had obtained for them an evil reputation.

Across the river, northward of Trichinopoly, lies the thrice-holy city of Srīrangam, which is rather a populated temple than a town *plus* a temple, for the houses are built within the three outermost of the five or six walled ambits of the pagoda. The permanent population is mainly Brahman, as one might guess from the comparative cleanliness of the place. The floating population is gathered from all parts of India, and now and again one may see there a devotee wandering stark naked through the indifferent crowd. Despite the walls and a superb, unfinished gateway, the great Vishnu temple is a disappointment. It possesses the usual stock of gems which, being uncut, are ineffective, and of ornaments which are in general of stereotyped and inartistic design. Indeed the most noticeable things in this collection are some large golden "chattis," or waterpots. But if the Vaishnavite temple possesses few architectural merits, the Saivite temple of Jambukēsvara, hard by, was, when I last saw it, fast climbing into the first rank. When I first went to Trichinopoly, this latter edifice, although much sanctity attached to it, was comparatively insignificant. Then the Nāttukkottai Chettis took it in hand. This group of Chettis has its headquarters in what is now the Rāmnād district, but has extended its trading transactions to Burma and its money-lending business to a great part of the south of the Presidency. It is an ill day for a village when the Chettis get their talons into it. By means of trade and loans they often amass great wealth, and so close is their spirit of fraternity that, as report says, every Nāttukkottai Chetti has the credit of the rest of the community behind him. They build in their homeland large houses, to be referred to anon, but they have elected to spend a great part of their wealth upon the renovation and beautifying of Saivite temples. In this latter operation they have, most fortunately, eschewed all modern abominations, such as plastered pseudo-classical columns, and follow scrupulously the Sāstras which lay down the principles of Dravidian temple-building in such detail that at the Jambukēsvara pagoda they found it sufficient to employ a "maistry" on forty rupees a month to supervise work costing lakhs of rupees. When I last visited the place, I found the improvements approaching completion. The new work is of the purest Dravidian type and in the best style. All the complicated grotesqueness of Tamil stonecraft is there, executed with such skill and patient toil in fine, hard stone that the result, in its richness and elaboration, does not fall far short of magnificence.

Tiruvellarai, a march farther on, is worth a visit because the temple possesses an unfinished gopuram which, though marred by the whitewash and red paint with which it is daubed (as religious edifices too often are), is a fine bit of work. The pagoda is surrounded by a grand wall the stability of which is threatened by rending vegetation.

The main northern road leads on to Pādalūr, near which is a hill. On this hill there was found the body of a boy, and a man was prosecuted for murdering him. The defence was that the boy had been killed by a panther. This was disbelieved and the accused was committed to the Sessions, where the evidence was held to be inadequate. Strange as it seems that the maulings of a wild beast should be mistaken for injuries inflicted in the course of a murder, there is some reason to suppose that the defence put forward was true, for soon after the trial a panther did kill on that knoll a woman and a boy from whose throats it sucked the blood.

The next camp beyond is Toramangalam, where I saw a man who had been bitten by a big bear which came into Kilipuliyūr village. The inhabitants tried to scare it away by shouting, but it rushed at the crowd, injured one man and killed another.

It is not very far on to Ranjangudi, where, on a high rock overlooking the tank, is the fine, bold fortress which witnessed during the French wars a panic among some of our besieging forces. Whilst I was encamped hereabouts, I received a petition marked by a singular precision of prediction. It was from a woman, who solicited my assistance on the night of the second day following the date of the petition when she anticipated that she would be ravished. I do not remember whether the poor lady's forebodings were fulfilled. More than once women less strict in their morals than that petitioner have appeared before me with written applications that I would certify officially that young and coy maidens accompanying them were old enough to do duty as dancing-girls.

If you strike westward from Toramangalam along the road which skirts the Pachaimalais, you reach

Turaiyūr, the abode of a Zamindāri family which, probably on account of a decline in fortune, kept itself so secluded that I never met any member of it. The place has little to show, but there is a handsome masonry tank and in the irrigation tank there stands a small, three-storeyed structure where the Zamindars used to sit and enjoy the air. This latter tank serves in the hot weather as a latrine for the village. It is connected with the stone tank, and in the rainy season supplies it with water which is drawn thence for drinking. Yet people survive in India.

Starting again from Toramangalam and moving eastward, one traverses the dismembered Zamindāri of Ariyalūr and an old sea-floor, one of the rare fossiliferous tracts of Southern India, and so reaches Udaiyārpālaiyam. Here the Zamindar came to visit me in state, attired in a green velvet coat embroidered with gold, white silk trousers with gold bands round the ankles, and a large, flat turban of gold thread carrying an aigrette adorned with emeralds and pearls. Of his followers, some were on horseback, and they wore peaked turbans of gold thread or head-dress of more antiquated design. This dignitary claimed to be the twenty-third Polegār of Udaiyār-pālaiyam, and, prior to the remote date of its settlement in that place, his family supplied, according to tradition, Polegārs to Conjeevaram. My return visit to this member of the old aristocracy was paid, in accordance with custom, on the same day. Painfully aware of the unimposing character of my own costume, I was met by retainers on horseback and afoot, an aged sick elephant, a baby elephant, and some camels. The Zamindar's house proved to be well worth a visit. It is the only inhabited specimen of an old Dravidian dwelling of the palace type which I have seen. The Darbar and Dancing Halls are ornamented with figures in plaster and wood and with designs which are not without a touch of barbaric richness. Amidst trash of the sort usually stored in Zamindars' houses, there was a bit of ivory-work wrought with extraordinary delicacy and ingenuity. It was probably Chinese, but the Zamindar bought it for two hundred rupees from a Kābuli who visited the village in a state of penury. On the way back from the house I passed the Siva temple on the edge of a fine tank which has a kiosque in it and is flanked on one side by à long, pillared corridor. It was dusk then, and the temple was only a vague and sombre shape encasing a block of blackness and a twinkling point of light.

Passing through Jayankondachōlapuram (Town of the Chōla who gained victory), I reached Gangaikandapuram, which probably stands for Gangaikandachōlapuram (Town of the Chōla who saw the Ganges). The outlying portions of the important but neglected temple here are much damaged. The inner shrine is, as usual, approached through a large, dark hall. The vimāna forms a pyramid of great size and is remarkable because (if I mistake not) it is constructed of stone throughout, and because of the boldness of its sculptural adornments. Some of these figures are of considerable size, and, although they are conventional in design and rough in execution, they are in certain cases rendered pleasing by the archly tender smile on their lips, a result perhaps of no conscious art on the part of the sculptor. It is difficult to understand how the immense blocks of granite or charnockite used in construction were lifted into position ; probably ramps of earth were used. It is said that all the stone used for the building of the temple had to be carried a distance of ten miles. There is, alongside the pagoda, a brickwork lion with a door in its breast, entering by which one comes on some dirty water which is supposed to flow underground from the Ganges.

I have been talking of Zamindars, and perhaps may mention that some of them have taken of late to literature, occasionally with results more curious than impressive. Every one who has dipped into Sanskrit literature knows its passion for classifying and subclassifying all things in Heaven and earth. This tendency affected the work of one of our Zamindar authors with rather comic effect. His book is entitled "On Heroes," and these he divided into twelve classes. Of these classes one consisted of "Heroes of Love," who are grouped under "Male" and "Female" and again subdivided into three genera. So we come to a discussion dealing in order, on the male side, with

(1) Husbands;
(2) Gallants;
(3) Whoremongers;

and, on the female side, with

(1) Wives;
(2) Neighbours' wives;
(3) Harlots.

In the southern half of the district by far the most agreeable halting-place is the Upper Anikat, where a clean and retired bungalow stands on the Kāvēri behind some splendid *marudai* trees. Waterfield nearly lost his life there. The river was running full when he went for a bathe. A mighty eddy seized him and span him round and round until he was upright in the vortex, when he was flung out of the whirlpool, exhausted but with just enough strength to reach the bank.

Waterfield's brother recited to me quite a good Irish bull. He and his sister were travelling in Ireland

and so nearly missed a train that one jumped into one carriage and the other into another. At the next station a ticket inspector asked the younger Waterfield for his ticket. "I am afraid I have not got it," he replied; "it is with my sister, who is in another carriage." "Ah, faith," was the response, "it's no matter. It's if you hadn't got a ticket that I should want to see it, but if you have, it's all right." Miss Waterfield once gave a party for Indian women, and one of the answers to her invitations deserves transcription: "I regret to say that my family consists of a kind of hysterical female who is not of a nature to enjoy your pleasures etcetera."

There are more Roman Catholic than Protestant missionaries in the district. The former, who are mostly French, live very humbly and indeed received then a stipend of only about thirty rupees a month. Nevertheless they have great influence with their flocks. I asked one of them whether he ever had trouble with his congregation, and he told me that, if such arose, he beat the offender hard with a stick and so secured peace and good behaviour. This example of benevolent tyranny recalls to my mind Widcombe, the Forest Officer, who gained great influence among the natives round Nilambur in Malabar. I cannot repeat the incident of Widcombe, the graciously apologetic Governor and the hustled carters, so will confine myself to mentioning an example of Widcombe's authority which a friend of mine witnessed. They were walking through the jungle when they saw on the other side of a river a stalwart Moplah. Widcombe shouted to him, and he plunged into the river and swam across. When he landed, Widcombe seized him and gave him a sound thrashing with his stick. At the conclusion of the ceremony the man salāmed, swam back, and went on his way, while Widcombe explained that the punishment had been inflicted on the Moplah for stealing some fowls from an old woman.

The Roman Catholics adopt in India their time-honoured policy of spreading the faith with the least possible disturbance of existing practices. Thus one may see in Trichinopoly regular Christian Car-Festivals, the great vehicle moving slowly and pompously through the village just as if the heathen god of the land were being honoured. The only ostensible difference is that the car carries the image of a Christian Saint instead of that of a deity, that it exhibits no obscenities, and that the carvings thereon represent angels and devils instead of dēvas and rākshasas.

One missionary whom I heard of, an American, founded a celibate sect in India. It fell to pieces when he married an Indian, but his austerities did not cease. Barefooted and bareheaded he wandered about the country living upon seven and a half rupees a month, though blessed with ample means. The true Apostolic spirit, but he went to such an extreme that none of his children was allowed to learn English until the age of fourteen lest his mind should be polluted by Western books, which may seem strange to those acquainted with some parts of Indian literature.

The subject of religious austerities leads my thoughts to privations undergone for less praiseworthy reasons. I shall not enlarge on the subject, but I feel that, as concerning meanness generally, a hint, a comment, and an instance are worth quoting as examples severally of delicacy, bitterness, and impudence. The first was tendered to old M., whose notorious stinginess made itself too evident in the state of his horses. One day, crawling along on a sorry nag, M. met the Master of the Ooty Hounds, who made some reference to the animal's appearance. On that, affecting much concern, M. begged for advice as to effecting an improvement. The Master, who was a doctor, cast an eye over the steed and, assuming his professional manner, replied, "Well, if I were you, I should try a tablespoonful of gram three times a day." Gram is, of course, the pulse which forms the staple food of horses in Southern India. So much for the hint. N., who was seriously ill, went to England with his wife, who was supposed to be miserly to a degree. Some people, gathered together, were discussing the case and one suggested that N. would never return to the East. "Return?" a man ejaculated, "of course he will return. Do you suppose that Mrs. N. would let him die in England when burial is so much cheaper out here?" So much for the comment. Now for the example, and I think all will agree that it would be hard to match it in the long record of dirty tricks. C. was employed by Newton, the lawyer, as his agent and was paid by commission on the sums passing through his hands. C. fell into debt, and Newton generously discharged his liabilities. When Newton came afterwards to examine C.'s accounts, he found that C. had credited himself with commission on the sum which Newton had given him to pay his debts.

I have strayed a long way from the southern part of Trichinopoly, but, in fact, it is not a very interesting country nor are the inhabitants attractive on the whole. Generally speaking, the Tamil is inferior in physique to the Telugu, and perhaps the southern part of Trichinopoly supplies the worst of the Tamil rural population. For the most part the people are ill-favoured and they are frequently of low facial type with that poverty of development which indicates an ungrateful soil and a scanty rainfall. They are a simple, backward folk. The women, who are often bare above the waist, flee helter-skelter at sight of a European, while the men will surround an encampment for hours, staring in silence at the tents. Among the lowest classes in some places a peculiarly ugly mode of salutation is in vogue. Crouching the body in an unseemly way, they utter a sort of guttural groan, "Oo-ahhh." Scattered about the country are a number of small Zamindars, or Polegārs, of the Tottiyār caste. Amongst them, I was told, not only is a man's wife common property to all his brothers, but even his father has access to her.

The decorations with which one is welcomed while on tour are, in Trichinopoly, particularly pretty, for they comprise, in addition to the usual mango leaves, coco-nut fronds, and plantain shoots, large cones formed of oleander blossoms strung together.

I have already mentioned that the district generally is wanting in picturesque features and touring is not so interesting as it is in many places. Still, away across the stony fields where the dewy stems of the castor-plants form a violet haze in the early light, there are to be found agreeable nooks and corners where a man may get through his day's office-work in peace and quietness; encamped, it may be, alongside an irrigation well, with a glimpse through the tent-door of empty red land sloping down to a clump of dark mango trees and up again to a naked, blistered hill. The Collector, in flight before Vakīls and petitioners, finds refreshment in such remote halting-places, especially at night when the dark earth yields no sound save the occasional lamentation of an owl.

It is when on tour that one learns best to appreciate the many admirable qualities of the Pariah servants.

I speak generally of course. I have seen documents and heard statements which suggest that not all Indian servants are deserving of commendation. But I like to find, for both good and bad, their testimonial in the record of that Indian " boy " who, mortally wounded by a shell in the Great War, spent his last breath in efforts to describe to his master the way to make that officer's favourite curry.

A party of snake-charmers came one day to my house, Fakīr's Tope, with baskets full of snakes alleged to have been caught in other compounds. There was the usual preliminary fooling with the snake-stone and the bitten man who showed a gashed finger, feigned nausea, and groaned and writhed so long as he was looked at. Then we adjourned to the compound, where four of the men, wearing only loin-cloths and turbans, but each carrying a blanket to throw over any snake seen, formed in line and advanced, producing upon their gourd-and-reed pipes those squeaky notes so well known to dwellers in India. These pipes contain horsehairs which are supposed to be affected by the proximity of snakes and, by change in their vibration, to produce an alteration of note which gives warning when one of these reptiles is near. The charmers put up out of the grass and caught four cobras and a fat Russell's viper. It was noticeable that these creatures, far from being attracted by the music, were all in full flight from it when seized, and I came to the conclusion that they were shaken out of the blankets as the charmers advanced. In order to test my opinion, I told the party to come again, but they failed to do so, and I cannot be positive that the snakes were introduced by their captors.

I saw only once a fight between a mongoose and a captive cobra. The mongoose kept on leaping at the reptile's nose, biting it and springing back until the snake's bleeding snout and obvious helplessness moved me, greatly to the disgust of its owner, to kill it. I then found that the fangs had been removed, and the charmer, interrogated, averred that, at the beginning of the fight, the mongoose invariably bites out the snake's fangs. I have heard of a case of a mongoose killing a dog. A man, accompanied by his terrier, called on a friend who owned a mongoose. The dog flew at the little animal, which seized it by the throat and held on until the dog, after rushing wildly about the compound for a time, dropped dead.

This chapter may close with a benediction invoked upon me at Christmastide by a resident of Trichinopoly who had doubtless some favour in view :

" Many happy returns of the season await you ! May the thorns of care never beset your path ! May peace be an inmate of your bosom and rapture a frequent visitor of your soul ! May the blood-hounds of misfortune never track your steps nor the screech-owl of sorrow alarm your dwelling ! May enjoyments tell your hours and pleasures number your days ! Blessed be he that blesses you and cursed be he that curses you ! "

CHAPTER XIII

PUDUKKOTTAI

THE Collector of Trichinopoly is *ex officio* Political Agent for the small Native State of Pudukkottai, which owes its continued existence to the foresight of a Polegār who backed the right horse in the race between England and France. The ruling family is of Kallan caste, but, in respect of language and habits, the Raja and his brothers might pass as Englishmen. The Raja himself married an Australian lady, and, on the occasion of his wedding, some well-meaning persons among his subjects sent him the following telegram : "Loving people of Pudukkottai send sympathy on Your Highness' marriage."

The Raja usually wears European costume, but on rare State occasions he may be seen magnificent in gold-embroidered white satin with jewels round his neck. The ancient ceremonial garb of the ruling family was probably, however, more correctly represented on the person of the Western Palace Jāghīrdār when he paid me a formal visit. He wore voluminous white muslin petticoats which two attendants held up in order to display the decorated shoes, a great, dish-shaped turban of gold tissue bearing a plume of black feathers, and, at the waist, a gold, or brass, hilted scimitar in a velvet sheath. He was accompanied by retainers carrying silver sticks and silver-handled chowries. The little old man might just have stepped out of an eighteenth-century picture ; a quaint and rather absurd figure.

The post of Agent was, for certain reasons, not quite a sinecure at that time, and I had to pay several visits to Pudukkottai town and also toured a bit in the State, which is a flat, monotonous tract. The capital lies thirty miles or thereabouts from Trichinopoly, and, when I paid it a visit, I travelled with relays of horses provided from the Raja's stables, that being in the days before Political Officers were forbidden to accept ordinary courtesies and hospitality from the chiefs to whom they are accredited. Pudukkottai reached, I was received with a salute of eight guns, housed in a comfortable bungalow, and soothed at meals by the Raja's band. The town is unusually well laid-out, a fact attributed to Sir William Blackburn, who, about 1825, induced the then ruler to pull down the small town and rebuild it on roomier lines. The place possesses a jail, which was then used also as a lunatic asylum, by no means to the advantage of either criminal or madman. The capital sentence is not passed in the State, and at that time no means for transportation were available. A life-sentence in a small jail must be an intolerable torture, and it was not surprising that one of the convicts who had been in prison for years for murdering his wife and mother-in-law begged me, as I passed round, to get him transported or hanged. The incident set in motion correspondence which resulted in better arrangements for both criminals and lunatics.

The reference to these latter unfortunates reminds me of one or two little incidents in which they played a part. Somewhere in Northern India there occurred a few years ago a series of derailments, or attempted derailments, of trains. Their cause was discovered and it was a strange one. The agent was a madman who had got into his head the whimsical notion that his Guru, or Spiritual Adviser, had taken to hiding himself in a railway engine. The disciple felt the loss of his Guru acutely, and conceived the plan of derailing locomotives until he should light upon the particular one chosen for concealment. When arrangements for a derailment were complete, the crazy searcher hid himself close by in readiness to pounce upon his evasive Preceptor as he issued from the overturned engine.

There was for many years in the Madras Asylum a harmless European patient, one B., to whom visitors were formally introduced by Captain M. the Superintendent. Tredegar, when making an official inspection, found the old gentleman somewhat ruffled. Pointing to the Superintendent, he observed, " This man is quite useless. I do not want to hurt Captain M.'s feelings, but I must repeat that he neglects his work. For instance, the bread and plantains which are supplied are disgraceful." Tredegar asked for samples of the things complained, and remarked, on the production of some plantains, that they looked all right. " What ? " cried the old man, falling back astonished, " What ? Do you call those plantains fit to set before the Holy Ghost ? "

At Tirumāyam there is a rather picturesque fort. It used to contain a good deal of armour, some of which has been removed to Pudukkottai. Among other things were hauberks and helmets composed of flat, iron ribs connected together by strips of chain-mail.

At Virālamalai, if I mistake not, I visited a temple which contains four large figures representing, as was said, certain ancient Polegārs of the Madura district. Here two plain, fat-hipped dancing-girls, pearls on head, trousers on legs, tinsel-cloths above, postured before me with quick tinkling of ankle-bells and clash of cymbals, to the throbbing of a drum and the squeaking of a bagpipe, and then I passed on to a cave in the rocky hill, where a filthy, matted-haired anchorite accepted eight annas from me. His holier colleague who occupied an adjacent cave was unfortunately absent, and I particularly wanted to see that person because of the peculiar diet which he affected. The Sub-Magistrate who accompanied and who informed me on the way that the use of soapnut as a cleansing material was dying out in the locality "owing to the introduction of enlightened soaps," assured me that he had seen that person make a meal of a handful of quicksilver mixed with two handfuls of green chillies.

A strange banquet, but Sanyāsis can do much worse than that. There happened in my time an inroad of Aghōra Pants into the Madras Presidency. These beastly ghouls used to dig up corpses in the burial-grounds and devour the putrid flesh. Whence the wretches came I do not know, and the police soon hustled them out of our area.

At Iluppūr, where I passed again into my own territory, there is another temple containing portrait statues, the figures being those of chiefs of the Nāyakkar dynasty. Hard by I found eloquent and painful testimony to the poverty of the tract in the shape of gaunt women with flat, hanging breasts, who were creeping about among the bushes in search of frogs to eat. The Jesuit missionaries work about here, and they seem to inculcate a good deal more ceremony and respect than do our Protestant pastors, if I may judge from my experience in one of these Jesuit villages, where the people bowed to the earth as I passed through and some of the women and children even knelt beside my path.

I shall end with an anecdote about a Native

State up Orissa way. It is hard to believe that it is a tale of twentieth-century India, but it is so and it is true. A sudden epidemic of murders in the State attracted the attention of the Government of India, who directed an inquiry which resulted in fastening the guilt on the Raja. It appears that cholera broke out in the capital of that amiable potentate, and he fell into such fear that he swore to offer, as the price of his own life, thirty-six human victims to the goddess Bowrini. In this country certain estates were held on "inām" tenure subject to the condition that the holders would supply offerings of human blood twice a year to the deity aforesaid. We may presume that this well-nigh incredible incident of tenure had not been enforced in recent years, but the Raja found it ready to hand for the attainment of his purpose. Orders went out to the ināmdārs to fulfil their duty, and the orders were obeyed. Victims were selected and disposed of, and their blood began to arrive in gourds and sections of bamboos at the palace of the Raja, who duly offered the consignments to Bowrini as they came in. Whether this monster had completed his vow before the Government of India stepped in I [illegible] not remember.

CHAPTER XIV

BURMA

WHILE stationed at Trichinopoly I paid a visit of a few weeks' duration to Burma, travelling from Madras in a steamer which contained 1800 coolies on their way to work in the rice-fields of that country.

At Rangoon the first thing visited was, of course, the Shwe Dagōn. It is nothing but a tall, gilded spire of queer shape rising from a circular base adorned with large bulbous "jewels," and abominable "Washington lights" do their utmost to vulgarize the place at night. Yet it satisfies some hunger of the mind because, incomprehensibly, it seems to belong to a visionary world where domes gleam against the blue and palaces throw up horned eaves and everything is beautiful, strange, and confused ; to the Orient, in fact, as it appeared to the youthful imagination of many of us. Probably the Shwe Dagōn owes a good deal of its fascination to the fantastic kiosques which, around the spire, taper into the semblance of flickering flames and display wood-carving in its ultimate perfection.

Having seen this and admired the stone dragons which writhe round the columns of the new Chinese joss-house and the glow of light and colour which fills after sunset the Street of Courtesans, I went on to Mandalay. This town stands in an unattractive champaign, and the disastrous influence of the West is only too apparent there in the use of Turkish towels as waist-cloths, of corrugated iron for the roofing of pretty wooden houses, and of coloured pictures from illustrated papers for the decoration of sanctuaries. The inhabitants, too, were a disappointment. They are not over-cleanly, and I missed the *bonhomie* of expression which I had expected of Burmese. They are, however, a sturdy enough people and their stout calves form a contrast to the thin shanks of India. Against such disappointments are to be set a wealth of notable buildings ; monasteries and pagodas with haunting names, wrought most beautifully and dazzlingly gilt. Sad it is that so much skill, taste, and toil should have been expended upon material so perishable as wood. A building which must not be overlooked is the King's Palace, which, for some time after the occupation, was used as the English Club. It is of wood, lavishly gilded, with a roof of great height borne upon noble posts of teak. The peculiar glass-inlay work of the country is freely employed there and has a brilliant effect. One of the most interesting things about the palace is the collection of royal robes, some of them truly regal in a charmingly bizarre fashion.

Beyond Mandalay a night in the train was followed by twenty-four hours in a river steamer. The boat was fitted forward with a saloon glazed on three sides to provide a good view ; the cabins were clean and comfortable. No pleasanter, idler mode of travel could be devised. Generally, too, the scenery is tame and monotonous which conduces to reposefulness. At Shwegu, however, the eye is caught by the glitter of a glass-inlaid column surmounted by a dragon, and in the Lower Defile the rugged, wooded banks demand continuous observation.

At Bhāmo the only object of interest, apart from the quaintly attired people, is the Chinese joss-house. ("Is" should, I fear, be "was," for it is said that the building has since been burnt down.) It contains a set of large figures upon whose countenances every vile and brutal passion is depicted with such abominable power as to leave one marvelling at the Chinese genius. In India we do not come in contact with the Chinese. In Burma I saw among them some fine, lusty bodies and some countenances expressive of a serene intellectuality which may or may not have been a reality. I conceive that it would be easy to learn to appreciate the Mongolian cast of feature.

On the return boat to Mandalay I had as companions some American tourists. They closed the venetian shutters of the deck-saloon and devoted their whole time to cards. A remark by one, "Burma is a side-show, and I do not want to see any more like it," seemed to meet with general approval. The beneficial effects of travel were similarly illustrated by a young Englishman who devoted two years to touring about the world for the stimulation of his intellect. Asked at the end of the time what he regarded as the most remarkable sight he had seen, he replied, after a little thought, "Well, do you know, I think the thing that struck me most was the way those fellows in Australia light a match in a gale of wind."

My last journey was to Gokteik in the Shān Hills, where a cold night was spent in a bungalow alongside a chasm which is spanned by a natural bridge about 550 feet above the floor of the glen. This bridge is in turn surmounted by a remarkable, spider-web-like railway bridge, of American design, 320 feet above it. The narrow cleft is eight or nine hundred feet deep. Its steep sides are covered with trees, and at the bottom is a clear, green stream which enters the great cavern formed by the natural bridge. The roof of the cave is hung with stalactites, and its floor is covered with stalagmites which form large cones or terraces with surfaces scooped into pools of limpid water. Admiration is equally divided here between Nature and the beautiful ingenuity of man.

I have met many English officials from Burma and never one who had not a word of praise for the Burmese. It is their *insouciance* which seems to be their particular charm. K. had occasion after an extensive flood to pay a visit to a Burmese landholder. The scene he came upon is this. On the unsubmerged top of a hillock was crowded the scanty undrowned remnant of the farm-stock; the house was under water to the eaves; on the ridge of the roof were seated the disconsolate housewife and her children; on the face of the waters the goodman was practising briskly for a canoe-race. In the Hindu, while there is not this *insouciance*, there is often a touch of rather engaging simplicity. MacIntyre met a man walking alone along a road, carrying in his hands a constable's turban and tulwar and on his head a large bundle. There ensued conversation. "What are you doing with that turban and sword?" "They are the constable's. I am a prisoner and he is taking me to the lock-up." "Where is the constable?" "He has stopped behind for a bit in the village over yonder. He will be coming along soon." "What is the bundle on your head?" "Oh, that is the stolen property." I had an experience of the same sort of *naïveté* myself. A visitor came bearing a certificate of success at the Pleadership examination. Without a voucher as to character he would not, however, be allowed to practise, and the object of his call was to get such a testimonial from me. "But," I objected, "how can I give you a character when I do not know you ?" "Not know me !" he exclaimed in surprise. "Why, your Honour dismissed me from the post of overseer in Trichinopoly." Then my memory went back to a scamp I had got rid of for dishonesty.

Such things provoke a sympathetic laugh, but the fact remains that, while, to the average Englishman, the average Burman is apparently congenial, the same cannot be said of the average Hindu, despite the latter's numerous estimable qualities. Many reasons may be suggested for this distinction, but undoubtedly the predominant one is the chilling and isolating influence of Caste. In certain places and among a certain class that form of social structure shows, for good or for ill, signs of disintegration, but, generally speaking, it is sound and rigid as ever. When I was in the Treasury at Trichinopoly I saw a retired peon come in to draw his pensionary pittance. I asked one of the clerks why the man was in such a shocking state of emaciation, and got the reply that the man's pension was insufficient for the purchase of food for himself as well as his children, and that, although the local Brahmans were quite willing to help him with food, he, being a Northern Brahman, was not permitted to touch it. So, between parental and ceremonial obligations, the man was just starving himself to death. There is more than a little fineness in that preference of lingering misery on earth to the risk of a spiritual stain. While I was in Trichinopoly I made a small private addition to the man's income, and this no caste scruple hindered him from accepting.

Well-meaning people often try to bridge the gap between European and Hindu by means of social gatherings comprising both races. It may be questioned whether they serve any useful purpose. They are certainly terribly boring to both parties. The irreverent speak of such entertainments as "East-and-Westers" and classify them as forms of the "Social Stunt" which they assert to be an invaluable instrument for the extraction of Honours, even to the extent of Knighthoods, from Governors of an earnest and "sympathetic" disposition.

I remember that when Tibbit went to South Arcot he found in existence there a Society to encourage friendly relations between Occidentals and Orientals which had been established by the wife of his predecessor. Through sheer inertia, I fancy, Tibbit continued the unifying festivities which were the main form which the activities of the Society took. The Scrymgeours went to stay with him about that time, and this subject cropped up in conversation. Tibbit maundered on, in the dreamy way he had, about the beneficial work which was being done until he got as tired of the topic as his audience and ended abruptly, "In short, Mrs. Scrymgeour, the object of the Society is the encouragement of sexual intercourse between Europeans and Natives." The verbal slip restored the company to cheerfulness.

The Burma trip over, I took the train for Trichinopoly at Madras. On the platform raged and shouted a white man in an ecstasy of rage. It was all because an order booking a seat had not been complied with, and the degree of passion developed as a consequence was quite extraordinary. The man, who was an American, got into my carriage and, when his anger had burnt itself out, proved to be an agreeable companion who descanted enthusiastically upon the beauty of Borneo, whence he had just come. At Chingleput I got out for dinner, but the American stated that it was not his intention to take anything to eat. I had the curiosity to ask whether he often dispensed with meals, and was amused by his answer : " Yes, I often go without food for a day, sometimes for two days, and once I had nothing to eat for three days. I find that fasting has a peculiar effect on me. I used once to have an ungovernable temper, but, since I took to occasional fasting, I have had it completely under control."

CHAPTER XV

MADURA

WHEN I took charge of Madura, it was a district of great size with a population of two and three-quarter millions. The eastern portion consisted of the great Zamindāris of Rāmnād and Sivaganga, to no small extent a roadless expanse of sand where travelling was difficult. The tract of black cotton-soil to the south formed the region of the Kallar people. The northern part was a more stony country bounded by hills and jungle. The western frontier was formed by mountains which in the Upper Palnis exceed 8,000 feet. To the central portion the Periyār Project has contributed irrigation, greatly to its enrichment and to the improvement of the Kallars holding land there in respect of their tribal tendency to steal. Strangely enough, the mass of the Kallars, though they regard theft as a reputable calling, are said to excel in truthfulness. They form, I believe, a self-governing community of unusual distinctiveness, owning allegiance to a chief whose decisions are final law. Their women frequently appear without the upper cloth, like many of the women on the West Coast, but they have not the pale-golden skin which renders the clean and shapely Nāyar women so attractive.

Madura Town lies on the Vaigai river, which is of the usual South Indian type, occasionally in turbid flood, more often a dazzling ribbon of white sand with here and there a runnel of clear water. The whereabouts of the town is indicated by the low, bare ridge known, for some reason or other, as Pasumalai or Cow-Hill, by the rock called Yānaimalai or Elephant Hill, which really does resemble that animal, and by the gigantic mass of black stone named Tiruparan-kunrram. The town contains over 100,000 people and is built on a rectangular plan which suggests that it was originally constructed within the walls, now vanished, of the temple in the middle. It is crowded and cramped and in certain parts and at certain hours particularly objectionable, the northern river-bank, the river-bed, and, at night, the streets being used as latrines, a practice difficult to check. There is a piped water-supply, but an inadequate one, and the river water is freely drunk by a people to whom bacterial infection would seem the wildest nonsense.

It is not, then, matter for surprise that cholera is always hanging about the place. What toll that disease took of young English life in bygone days is apparent from cemeteries and scattered tombstones. Now it is comparatively rare among Europeans, and the towns are being gradually rendered safe by the introduction of water-supply systems. It remains, however, a terrible scourge. I saw a long while back a reprint in an Indian newspaper of an old poem which is supposed to have been written by one Bartholomew Dowling at a time when his regiment was writhing under the lash of cholera. It struck me as somewhat remarkable, but I will quote only two of the verses :

" There's many a hand that's shaking,
There's many a cheek that's sunk,
But soon, though our hearts are breaking,
They'll burn with the wine we've drunk.

So stand to your glasses steady,
'Tis here the revival lies.
A cup to the dead already,
Hurrah for the next that dies.

"Who dreads to the dust returning?
Who shrinks from the sable shore
Where the high and haughty yearning
Of the soul shall sting no more?
No, stand to your glasses steady,
The world is a world of lies.
A cup for the dead already,
Hurrah for the next that dies."

There is more to be seen in the city of Madura than in any other town of Southern India. The great temple of Sundarēsvara and Minākshi is of much interest. Its principal feature is the statuary which is less conventional and, so, more lifelike than usual. One group of figures attains somewhat of the terrible which is rare among the works of Dravidian sculptors, who, when they aim at horror, commonly produce only ugliness. Some of the best or, at all events, most ornate of the stonework is quite modern, such as the Kambhattadi mantapam, a particularly rich mass of carving. The outside of the pagoda is unimpressive. It is roofed over to an unusual extent, the roof being pierced by the vimānas over the principal shrines. In most large Dravidian places of worship the darkness of the interior produces an oppressive sense of mystery. Here this effect is pronounced, for the gloom is in places profound and the golden flame before the idol seems illimitably far.

You emerge into sunlight when you reach the Golden Lily tank, the beauty of which resides mainly in its name. The stone basin is filled with water of the filthiest sort. I do not know whether it is drunk, but, judging by its appearance, surmise that the pious appreciate it as a beverage. Round the tank is a cloister the walls of which are painted with horrid scenes of impalements and other tortures inflicted on the Jains or Buddhists, scenes incongruous with the character of a people naturally averse from cruelty and violence.

Among the temple treasures are a number of stones which, if sapphires as stated, must be of considerable value, for they vary from about half an inch square to nearly double that size. In the hoard, which is generally uninteresting, is a gold plate presented by that remarkable old Collector, Mr. Peter. He was known as Peter Pāndya among the people, the Pāndyans being a very ancient dynasty of the south, and like a king he ruled. To do this he needed money, and such he found by borrowing from the Government Treasury. When he realized the extent of his indebtedness, he tried to make good by instructing his Sheristadar to trade with the public money in his charge, but he died with a considerable balance against him, protesting at the end his innocence of fraudulent intention.

Frauds on the Treasury still happen from time to time, and in one case they involved a Collector in very heavy loss. At that period the rupees were stored in canvas bags, and P., the incoming Collector, contented himself, when taking over charge of the Treasury, with counting the bags. Unfortunately the silver contents had been replaced by copper in many instances, and I believe that P. had to make good to the extent of a lakh of rupees. Net bags for silver coins were introduced as a result of this occurrence.

Before passing to the other public buildings of Madura, I may make a brief reference to the village shrines which abound in Southern India and strike the eye by reason of the rough representations, in clay or whitewashed brick, of horses and elephants, sometimes over life-size, which are ranged beside them, along with iron spears or tridents, points uppermost. The figured animals are dedicated to the use of Aiyanār, who goes a-hunting on them at night, armed with the weapons provided at the spot. Riding one day towards such a shrine situated in a grove, I was besought to turn aside and, on asking the reason, was told that the deity will not tolerate in his neighbourhood any rival equestrian and that, if I passed his temple on horseback, he would smite the adjacent village with cholera. I dismounted, of course, though I had ridden past scores of shrines elsewhere without protest. I heard of a European official climbing on to a brick elephant beside a shrine of Aiyanār and taking his seat on it. The marvellous tidings that the god had deigned to visit the place in full light of day flew round the village and an excited crowd poured out. When they found out what had actually occurred, they were seized with fury and chased the stranger away with stones and revilings. He, on his part, lodged a complaint before a magistrate, but, on learning that he had unwittingly wounded the religious feelings of the people, he withdrew the charge and apologized.

To return to Madura. Opposite the big temple is the largest mantapam of Southern India, an oblong, wall-less, stone structure known as Pudumantapam or Tirumāl Nāyak's Choultry. It is just over a hundred yards long, and the flat stone roof is supported by many pillars adorned with the customary figures, on a large scale, of rearing horses and of the monsters known as Yālis. It is a striking example of Tamil architecture.

Tirumāla Nāyakkar, who reigned in the seventeenth century, has left, in addition to the mantapam, a remarkable palace which is still used as a Court-house. The outer courtyard, whatever may be the professional view of its style, is extraordinarily imposing by reason of the vast columns, of European type, which flank it. Behind lies the Darbar Hall, a peculiar combination of Dravidian and Western styles. The effect is heavy, but this is atoned for by the originality and strangeness of the design. Some distance from the palace is the handsome, square, stone-built tank known as the Teppakulam (Teppam means a raft, and most temples of any size have a raft-tank for the performance of a ceremony in which a raft plays a part). The tank is, for a temple tank, of great size, but its happiest feature is the group of white structures on the square islet in the middle. The central building is a six-storeyed pavilion, and at each corner stands a little kiosque. If you choose, you can cross to the islet on an impromptu raft supported by earthenware pots, but the only result will be that lovely edifices of perforated marble embowered among trees and shrubs are degraded into whitewashed brick and plaster.

Near the tank is the famous banyan tree in a garden which was once regularly rented by the District Judge, but afterwards came again into the hands of the Zamindar who owns it. Old descriptions of the banyan of India exaggerated its size, though they could hardly exaggerate its beauty and utility as an avenue tree, but in this particular case the magnitude almost realizes the expectations of the inexperienced. Its branches extend over a rough circle the diameter of which is about a hundred yards, but this result was not attained, as I was informed by Sir Philip Hutchins, long well known as Judge of Madura, without a lot of care and trouble on his part. There is another very fine banyan at the public bungalow at Mēlūr with a shade diameter of nearly eighty yards. The banyan is always a delight to those who care to watch the busy life of bird, reptile, and insect which focuses in it.

Across the river lies the Collector's house, the Tumkum, which also is attributed to Tirumāla Nāyakkar. The core of the edifice is a mound, probably artificial, and, seen from a distance, the building rises baronially above its surroundings. It is a singular place, full of ghostly shadows. The moonlight, pouring into the main room, breaks against forty square pillars whence spring cinquefoil arches. From the point of view of lighting and furnishing it was my wife's despair. To the three-floored original structure the Public Works Department have added a wing of an uncompromising, rectilinear order.

There is, finally, the Perumāl temple with its adjunct the Lakshmi temple. The lower part of the former is sumptuously ornamented in bold relief, but it is the latter which gave me the more pleasure. I saw it under unusually favourable conditions, for, the temple being out of use owing to reconstruction, I was able to inspect the penetralia which in ordinary circumstances are closed to Europeans. If the fine, gray, crystalline stone called charnockite is worked over with oil and iron filings, it takes a glossy, jet-black surface, very handsome. The new shrine in the Lakshmi temple is made of this stone so treated, is shaped on most harmonious lines, and is decorated richly but with fine restraint. The encompassing pillars are well carved, and their grayness contrasts very pleasingly with the blackness of the mausoleum-like central structure. The whole a noble piece of workmanship.

A couple of miles or so from Madura is the forbidding and stupendous crag already referred to as Tirupārankunrram. At the top is a mosque, in the sides are cells for anchorites, but the main thing is the temple at the foot. It impressed me enormously, perhaps beyond reason, but the gigantic portal and ponderous doors might well give entrance to the Pit, and inside, in those obscure spaces, is there nothing? What slinks behind the distorted outline of that pillar? What, in that pitchy recess, stinks and gibbers and stirs the hot, greasy air with flabby membranes? Is it only a bat, think you?

A slightly longer excursion takes one to Alagarkōvil whose god visits Madura periodically to wed Minākshi. The temple is hardly worth noticing, but the clump of hills behind rises to 2,000 feet, and contains some unusually large mahogany trees as well as a herd of bison, which is protected from the sportsman but not, unhappily, from rinderpest.

In the bed of one of the tanks near the Tumkum is held yearly a great cattle fair whereat, sometimes, 20,000 beasts are, as they say, assembled. At that spot is also performed the Jellikat, one of the few "manly sports" indigenous to Southern India and apparently confined to this district. Cloths are wrapped round the horns of bulls, and young men who seek honour strive to snatch the cloths away. The game is fairly interesting to watch, but not so much so as I expected, for the bulls seemed rather vexed than infuriated and their charges were somewhat perfunctory. When a charge occurred, the men in the way, if they could not readily escape, just threw themselves flat, and the bull skipped over them, never attempting to gore the prostrate bodies. This would be a useful bit of knowledge to possess, if one could be sure that all bulls have the like habit.

On the lowlands of Madura the best climate is owned by Dindigul, which possesses also one of those gigantic rocks so characteristic of the Indian Peninsula,

This bears the remains of a fort which was garrisoned in the early days of our occupation, but proved, as they say, to be so malarious that the troops were shifted. This is curious, for Dindigul town is as free from fever as any place in the Peninsula. I had my first experience of plague on a large scale at Dindigul and Palni. Trouble threatened at the former, the people being naturally annoyed at the prospect of being driven out of their houses into a temporary encampment. I had to hurry to the place and applied the lenitive of a general meeting at which I talked about germs in language as simple as I could command. At the end of the discussion the Kāzi laid his hand indulgently on my head and uttered a blessing over me, which was good of him, for, of course, neither he nor anybody else believed a word I had said. In fact, a missionary told me afterwards that a person of some position in the town was spreading the story that the officials had started the plague-scare in order to provoke a riot and so get an opportunity to kill people. It was more to the point that I promised to evict no one who got himself and his family inoculated. There was a great rush thereupon to the inoculators and the epidemic was soon stayed. The same plan was followed with similar success at Palni. There was no such *contretemps* as thwarted Lascelles' efforts on a similar occasion. He called a general meeting in a stricken town, spoke strongly for inoculation, and even had himself inoculated *coram populo*, but he failed to arouse enthusiasm, for the audience knew well that the dose administered to Lascelles was merely water, whereas for others a lethal brewage was ready. However, in the end, Lascelles' impassioned appeals induced a stalwart cooly to come forward. This valiant fellow, for he was all that to face the horrible, imaginary risk, no sooner felt the prick of the needle than he fell down in a swoon, and against the ensuing panic entreaties were of no avail.

Neither at Dindigul nor at Palni was there any disturbance of the peace, and the only place in the district where rioting occurred in my time was a village on the coast, where the fishermen, as they rose in the world, had been growing resentful of their thraldom to the Muhammadan Labbais. A show of discontent led to an attack by the Labbais, who burnt down nearly the whole village. The fisherfolk, however, escaped out to sea, and the affair ended in the quartering of punitive police on the Labbais and the collection of compensation from them.

Some said that Madura was seething with sedition at that period, but I saw no signs of it. Perhaps my eyes would have been opened had I roamed the bazaars at night in disguise. Perhaps not. I have heard of several Europeans who tried to gain information in this way, but they were always detected with ease, and their motive for assuming disguise was generally lamentably misinterpreted.

The possession of a hill-station 7,000 feet above the sea makes Madura a crowned queen among the districts. The road to this Elysium, through Periyakulam, has from time immemorial had an evil reputation for highway robbery. One of my earliest recollections of Madras is seeing at a dinner-party Sparsholt of the Board of Revenue with his head swathed in bandages. The then Collector of Madras was Sneyd. Both Sparsholt and Sneyd were tall, personable men, and the latter had that quality of sinister beauty which one associates with the Master of Ballantrae. Between the two men there was ill-will, and when Sparsholt was knocked about by dacoits in Sneyd's district, he conceived the idea that his assailants were the henchmen of a certain Zamindar whom Sneyd was using as an instrument of his rancour. A criminal case developed out of the matter and reached the High Court. The proceedings there did not end as Sparsholt wished, and from that time forward he regarded the Chief Justice with loathing and contempt, solacing himself at times with the surmise, poignant with unexpressed desire, that that dignitary was drinking himself to death.

Buckle was another European who suffered a dacoity, though not in Madura. The cart in which he was travelling was stopped by a rope across the road and he jumped out into a gang of men, from one of whom he wrested a stick. The man bolted with Buckle in pursuit, hitting at him. The fugitive fell down and the pursuer fell over him. The rest formed a ring and pelted Buckle with stones until his arm was broken and he lay unconscious and bleeding. When he came to, he started on a painful tramp of seven miles to Pollāchi. Arriving at the toll-bar, he begged for water, but the turnpike man took him for a devil on its rounds and had no disposition to attend to his wants. He crawled on to the Travellers' bungalow, where he got help. He was ill for a long time afterwards.

There was no driving-road to Kodaikānal at the period I am talking about; only a steep bridle-path up which women were carried in chairs, while men usually rode the little "tats," or country ponies, which look so miserably weak and thin but can go such extraordinary distances. The lower part of the path traverses a feverish zone of forest, an object of such solicitude to the Forest Officers that Eyre posted up a universally ignored notice requesting gentlemen not to smoke when passing through it, while Dumbleton inserted in the coupe-leases a condition binding lessees to forbid their coolies from easing themselves therein "in order to prevent the spread of prickly-pear." A long, hot ascent by "the zigzag" ends in a region of tree-fern and bracken; the Roman Catholic seminary at Shembaganūr is passed, and, after a last, sharp rise, bungalows scattered round a hill-encircled lake are revealed.

The house which I occupied here stands at the edge of a mighty cliff across the face of which a small stream throws a ribbon of foam. Far below the hills and plains of Madura glow in the sunlight. The owner of the house was Bewley, who will be remembered by many as an omnivorous reader and a book-collector of such ardour that, in his Madras abode, his bed occupied a small clearing reached by a lane through a waist-deep undergrowth of volumes. He had not neglected to stock his Kodaikānal residence also on a generous scale, for the books there were reputed to number twenty-five thousand and may have been half as many. Of such a mass of literature it was inevitable that a portion should be unsuitable for the family circle, and that was so even during my tenancy, which was after the library had passed through the winnowing hands of Gandy. That gentleman, when previously occupying the house, took the opportunity to remove the volumes which he thought unfit for perusal, and, embarking with the objectionable works, he discharged them into the lake. Bewley was, not unnaturally, indignant at his tenant's conduct and used to declare in the freest terms his conviction that the books had not been destroyed as alleged. In this I am sure that he did grave injustice to Gandy, because, soon afterwards, Gandy issued a circular enjoining upon his subordinates the strictest purity of life, even to the extent of eschewing all entertainments at which dancing-girls were present, for, as he very properly observed, "we must avoid the very appearance of Evil."

Kodaikānal is frequented by missionaries to such an extent that a wit divided society there into Kodaicarnal and Kodaispiritual. Many of these missionaries are Americans of the Madura district, and it was one of them who told me that, on the occasion of the death of a Christian from snake-bite at Mēlūr, the kinsfolk of the deceased refused to bury the man until they had ascertained that he himself was not prepared to view the corpse and restore it to life by the exercise of his spiritual powers.

A good time ago a missionary whom I knew was much exercised over a drought which was affecting part of the country. He considered that the Government were treating the situation too lightly, and communicated to a home paper some pictures of the alleged victims of starvation. They attracted the attention of the Secretary of State, who brought them to the notice of the Madras Government. An enquiry elicited the fact that the pictures were reproductions of photographs taken in a real famine of earlier date. The missionary's motives hardly justified his act in the opinion of most people.

Kodaikānal, which possesses an observatory where solar work is done by a well-known astronomer, stands on a plateau somewhat resembling that of the Nīlgiris, but the sweeping, grassy hills have not been grazed and trodden smooth by generations of buffaloes and are too rough for galloping. There are some neat bungalows to put up in, some rounded holts to diversify the landscape, and always fresh, clean air and wide-spreading views of hill and plain.

A pathway which has since been merged in a road giving access to the plains used to drop from Kodaikānal in the direction of the outstanding cone of Perumāl, then cross Neutral Saddle, and, a little way beyond, creep round the face of a cliff, at which point it consisted of planks stayed to the rock. This was not a nice bit, and a high official has been known to do the passage on all-fours. On the other hand, one daring person tried to accomplish it on horseback, but in the middle the animal stopped and began to tremble violently. The rider had hardly time to slip off before the horse rolled over the edge and was killed. After a descent of three or four thousand feet, the old path debouched into a country very different from that in which it started, for it had then reached the plateau of the Lower Palnis ; a rough region clothed with a thick jungle in which the cardamom spice flourishes and with the rank growth of abandoned coffee estates. The place produces some very fine trees and any quantity of fever. Having crossed this shaggy tableland, one descends by bridle-paths, and so, in two or three stages, reaches Palni, where are to be found a temple of much sanctity and a water supply which, through the agency of an unceasing current of pilgrims, serves effectively to diffuse cholera over a considerable part of the Presidency.

One often meets far afield the pilgrims making for Palni, carrying on their shoulders those flat poles with a burden slung from each of the upturned ends which are known as "kāvadis." What exactly the pilgrims carry on these poles I am not certain ; offerings to the god Subramanya presumably. I met a European Police officer who performed one of these pilgrimages along with a party of Nāyars from Malabar. They took him readily, and, wearing similar costume and sharing their food, he accompanied them to the temple, into which he was admitted, unnoticed or, at all events, unchallenged, as a worshipper.

The chequered career of another Police officer, one Blewitt, perhaps merits a passing allusion. I met him first in India and next leading the life of a man of fashion in London. On his return to India from this golden spell of leave, he went to see the Inspector-General of Police to ask him for the post of Assistant Commissioner of Madras. At this interview he enlarged to his astonished Chief upon his desire to secure the amenities of metropolitan life for a married lady who had fallen in love with him, closing his address with the words, " She is coming out to me and, as soon as her husband divorces her, I shall marry her. She will like Madras better than up-country, and she really is tip-top." The lady did not, in fact, come out to Madras, though it is said that her boxes arrived, and Blewitt consoled himself for the disappointment by taking into his charge another married woman. This step, combined with unauthorized absence from his district, led to his removal from the service. After that, through a series of episodes, he quickly faded off the scene of Indian life.

The repair of the temple at Palni led to a dispute as to the class of the community which had the right to replace in position the stūpi, or apical ornment, of the building, and feeling ran so high that my presence seemed necessary. I found that the situation had been exaggerated, but, as both parties clamoured to be heard, I devised a means of satisfying them without subjecting myself to a long wrangle over details of ritual. The temple stands on a hill and is approached by a long and tiring succession of flights of steps. I announced to the Vakīls, or counsel, for both parties that I was about to visit the temple, and that they could expound their respective cases to me on the way up. By the time I was halfway up both Vakīls had intimated that they had completed their addresses. So the contending parties were satisfied, and they came to some amicable arrangement or other.

When Ramsay of the Railway and I were in a boat off Mantapam in the Pāmban Straits, he looked round at the sea, the flat, scattered islets, the long spit of sand with a mantapam at the point and the palmyras growing here and there, and remarked that the scene was just like a picture out of some old mission book on India. I can give no better description of it.

This shallow water between India and Ceylon is a treasury of pearls and a museum of marine zoology. There is said to be good seer-fishing, but, though I went out several times after that dashing fish, I never caught any. Occasionally a dugong is brought ashore, and, just before my first visit to Pāmban, a whale, twenty-eight feet long, got into shallow water there and was killed and cut up for the oil.

Of the islands in these parts Rāmēsvaram, or Pāmban, Island is much the biggest. The village of Pāmban is unhealthy and has nothing to offer to the sightseer, except the diving-bell used for cutting a passage for ships through the coral reef which connects the island with the mainland, and now carries a great railway bridge. There is always a drift of ships past the island, mostly square-rigged vessels of a few hundred tons built at Colombo, things of wistful beauty as seen from the shore.

The greater part of the island is an undulating desert of bleached sand. A railway line crosses it to the famous temple of Rāmēsvaram, the main feature of which is its great corridors. These extend to an enormous length. Their flat roofs are upheld by square pillars with the heads of grinning monsters for brackets. There is no variety of style, but the size and strangeness of these cloisters render them imposing.

From the colonnade at the back I caught a glimpse of the shrine with its glimmering lights. It looked immensely distant, and here and there a sunbeam, splitting the intervening obscurity, struck a flame from a golden-hued patch of metal. The occasional clang of a bell or harsh bray of a conch, the uncouth shapes in stone half-seen in the shrouding darkness, the illusion of great space, bestow upon this part of the temple a solemnity with which mingles a suggestion of cruelty as if, in the murk recesses of the building, bloody sacrifices were being furtively offered.

I visited the place with Spankie as my companion, and we were met at the station by a band of priests who conferred upon us the paravattam by binding muslin shawls round our heads. We were then heavily laden with garlands of flowers and tinsel. The musical instruments struck up, palm-leaf umbrellas were raised above our heads, and so we advanced towards the temple in great state. The fillet tied round Spankie's head soon slipped over one eye and his appearance became very singular indeed. But, in fact, Indian modes of personal adornment do not go well with European clothes. A few miles beyond Rāmēsvaram the railway attains Dhanushkodi, at the end of the sandspit which points to Ceylon. This is a spot to which pilgrims throng, because a bathe in the sea there is efficacious for the removal of sin.

A tragic incident occurred about this time in connection with the islands of the neighbourhood. A party of eleven Mussalmāns from the north who were over in Ceylon wanted to return to their homes. They had got into their heads the erroneous idea that, if they travelled in the ordinary way, they would be detained in a plague-quarantine camp on arrival in India, so they hired a sailing boat and left Ceylon at night, with intent to be landed secretly on Rāmēsvaram Island.

At dawn they were off a shore which the boatmen, probably in a hurry to be gone, but perhaps in good faith, declared to be that of the island in question, and the northerners landed and started to walk to Rāmēsvaram village, which they understood to be about five miles off. After walking half a mile or so, they discovered that they were on a deserted, sandy islet, a mile or so from the main island. There are always plenty of boats moving about in the Straits, and it is difficult to understand how the party failed to attract attention, but fail they apparently did. The first victim was a boy, who was drowned in trying to swim to the main island. The rest resigned themselves to the agonies of hunger and thirst, and when, ten days afterwards, a fisherman sighted the unhappy people, only six were alive. The skipper of the boat was prosecuted in Ceylon and convicted of rash and dangerous navigation, or some such offence, but I do not suppose that the conviction was upheld on appeal.

These islands and the adjacent coast appertain to the great Zamindāri of Rāmnād, the proprietor of which bears the hereditary title of Raja. Its chief town, of the same name, is a disagreeable place through which cholera sweeps ever and again. In one of its visitations it quenched the vivid life of Hawke, of the Survey Department, who left his widow in such bad circumstances that a general subscription was started among his European friends, which meant every one who knew him. The sum raised was, I believe, R. 30,000, and, although that did not go far towards the purpose in view, it was much more, I am certain, than would have been collected for anyone else.

At Rāmnād lies the talented Francis Ellis, a Civilian who died in 1817. An epitaph record his merits in English and Tamil. The English version, which alludes to his "playful disposition" and energy in work, is graceful and appropriate, and the Tamil version, too, is said to be in the best style. Ellis was an Orientalist and had gathered a great store of manuscripts which it was his intention to publish, but they say that he had made a resolution not to start on his great work until he reached the age of forty, and, just before doing so, he was accidentally poisoned. It is also said that for months his successor's cook used the precious hoard for lighting the kitchen fire.

At the headquarters of the adjacent large Zamindāri of Sivaganga there is an interesting collection of weapons, which includes double-pointed daggers made of antelopes' horns, a bow of great size, and, strange link perhaps with Australia, some of those boomerangs which were, and possibly still are, in use among the Maravars. From Sivaganga town I went to Nātēsankottai to see some of the houses, occupied by Nāttukkottai Chettis, for which the locality is famous. Those which I saw were decorated outwardly with glaring colours and plaster figures. One which I entered contained good carving in wood and the interior walls were glossy with that nice, clean "shell-chunam" which used to be largely employed in the construction of European houses in Madras. There were lots of little pictures, religious or discreetly amorous, and hundreds of those tinted glass balls which, with musical-boxes and, nowadays, gramophones, afford such delight to the unsophisticated Hindu of means. The bedrooms were minute cells without light or air, and intolerably hot. Many of these houses have private electrical installations, and large sums are often spent upon the erection of them. House inspection over, I visited the temple, where I received the paravattam and the sacred ashes of burnt cow-dung, whilst a dancing-girl threw saffron-water at my feet to ward off the evil eye. The Nāttukkottai men wear nothing above the waist, not even on their shaven heads, and are a stolid-looking set, black and often portly. The women carry peculiar, heavy ornaments, and the tāli, or token of wedlock, worn by the married ones is of unusual size.

Both these Zamindāris are inhabited to a large extent by Maravars, a class which seems to be particularly prone to the commission of murders. Several cases of unusually savage crimes on the part of these people occurred in my time, and in one instance a party of them, after killing the Karnam, or Accountant, of their village, cut off his head and paraded the streets carrying it stuck on a pole.

Although predominantly Tamil, the district contains both Canarese and Telugus. These last are mostly Reddis, a caste, in local opinion, equally competent as husbandmen and complaisant as husbands. It is said to be settled custom with them to abstain from entering their homes when the presence of a pair of shoes at the door shows that the housewife is closeted with a lover. In the Varushanād Valley there are to be found, or were until lately, people who procure fire by friction. I regret that I know very little about the inhabitants of the district, for it is doubtless very interesting ethnologically. My excuse is that I was absorbed in contemplation of the activities of sundry minor officials "wearying themselves to commit iniquity."

Official business took me away from Madura for a time and carried me to Simla, a town with a singularly makeshift, unsubstantial look, perched upon a gigantic slag-heap, a term which seems to describe as aptly as any the dingy foothills of the Himālayas. The place was then still full of the story of a dramatic performance given by the Viceroy's children. The play, which was understood to have been composed by the children, related to the separation of a wife from her husband whom cruel fate, or inclination, drove to roam abroad for a long term of years. The *dénouement* represented the return of the wanderer with a full account, E. and O. E., of his adventures. His spouse listened with wifely patience to the recital and then, rising with dignity, exclaimed, "And, in the meantime, I too have not been idle." So saying, she swept aside a curtain and revealed a group of children of all ages.

I returned to Madura to learn there of the death from poison of a French artist who, though I was previously unaware of it, had long been living in great poverty in the bazaar. He left behind him a collection of pictures which was afterwards sent to relatives in France, and a letter expressive of disappointment over the past and despair for the future. This notwithstanding, a verdict of accidental death was returned.

I was engaged in planning a trip to Jaffna by sailing-boat and a shooting excursion to the High Wavy Mountains, when there arrived the summons to headquarters which closed my district life. I left with regret, although the burden of my duties in Madura had been such as to demand some such valedictory gift as another outgoing collector received along with the following letter:—

"God save our District Magistrate.

"Honoured Sir, I beg you to accept as kindly gifts in departing 5 pomegranate fruits, 5 oranges, 2 dozen walnuts, and 1 bottle hair-lotion. The latter is restorative to hair and invaluable after much toil to weak brain."

CHAPTER XVI

A VOL D'OISEAU

IN my last phase I had the opportunity of getting a fleeting glimpse of the whole Presidency, and this chapter will contain the remarks which it occurs to me to make about places not dealt with before.

When I reached Madras from Madura, the agitation caused by the circular letter issued by the Reverend Anthony Smatters to the young Englishmen of Madras was subsiding. That epistle enlarged upon a certain text in Thessalonians with such copiousness and vigour as to arouse curiosity, and earnest enquirers, who set to work to investigate the subject, announced that the house occupied by the minister and his consort stood in a compound containing several other dwellings, one of which was occupied by a woman of light reputation. It was reported, as possibly bearing upon the tone of the epistle, that the propinquity of the two houses had resulted in several regrettable mistakes.

So I was informed by the Director of Agriculture, a gentleman of humorous turn, concerning whom certain aggrieved ryots, memorializing the Board of Revenue, remarked, "Presenting petitions to him is like playing music before a buffalo." It was in that officer's time that the Department of Agriculture came to life after its long cataleptic trance in the Limbo where paper departments lead their half-sentient existence. In its earliest days the Department, which might have found a suitable device in the words "Rusticus expectat," consisted of a single Agricultural Expert who was kept quiet in the office of the Board of Revenue by supplies of inaccurate statistics. The Revenue Divisional Officers used to furnish some of these in the form of reports on the outturn of various crops as ascertained by personal experiments. Cholmondeley gave me a proof of the worthlessness of these returns. He had taken a lot of trouble over three of the outturn experiments before he left his Division, and was annoyed later to find that the Board had rejected the results obtained by him as untrustworthy. On the other hand, that authority had commended two other experiments in his name as affording valuable information. As Cholmondeley had never made these other experiments, he wrote to the head clerk of his former office for an explanation. The answer he got ran : "Your Honour made only three experiments, but, as the rules require that five shall be made, we made up in the office suitable figures for two other experiments and sent them to the Board." The wife of the Agricultural Expert referred to above underwent the unusual misfortune of being struck by lightning and, although she was not killed, her health was permanently affected. I have heard of other instances among Europeans of injury due to the same cause. A curious case was that of two children of the T.s who, with their ayah, were struck while on the Kudiremukh. The boy lost strips of skin from his back. The girl had a hole neatly drilled through her hand, and the ayah suffered like the girl. The children recovered, but their attendant died of tetanus.

As nominal head of the Agricultural Department, I was approached by a German baron with a scheme for improving the supply of natural indigo to enable it to compete with the synthetic dye. Assistance from public funds was given, but the experiment proved a failure and aroused doubts as to the baron's *bona fides*. His subsequent career was disastrous. His then wife was his fourth, rumour having it that the first died, the second was divorced, and the third bigamously remarried. He and the lady then received as his wife got a young girl possessed of some means under their influence, and it needed the intervention of the German Consul to remove her from a companionship which was proving unduly expensive to her. The baron, possibly as a consequence of this intervention, fell into financial difficulties while at Ootacamund and, being besieged by incensed creditors, made a bolt through a side door for Fern Hill Station, but a bailiff was on him before he could board a train. What followed I do not know, but soon afterwards the baron was back in Europe with the police on his track for bigamy or trigamy. It all ended with a suicide at Antwerp.

I have not hitherto made any allusion to the annual Fine Arts Exhibition at Madras. Just a word may be permitted. Of late years artists with futurist tendencies have invaded it and contributed works of such a remarkable character as to move, one year, a facetious person to send in a caricature of their style. To his great surprise the committee accepted it as a serious work and even accorded to it "Honourable Mention." The pictures exhibited by the Southern Indians are often amazingly bad, in fact hardly rise above the art of the nursery ; they are greatly inferior on the average to the works of Indians from farther north. One of these last stays in my memory by reason of its quaint superscription. The subject of the picture was two beggars with a baby, and it was thought necessary to explain it by appending the following verse :—

> " Remote Ful moon black blue sky
> Sheds her lustre silver shy.
> Her benighted begging couple,
> Alas the baby under grapple."

And now I must start on my Grand Tour, but I may very well fill in the minute before the train starts with the recital of an instance of sturdy racial prejudice which recurs to my memory.

The first Indian Judge of the High Court was Muttuswāmi Aiyar, whom I always heard spoken of as a good judge and worthy of respect in other ways. The door-keeper of his Court-room was an old soldier. Wright, the solicitor, passing the door of that room and hearing a voice droning within, asked the door-keeper what was going on. The answer was, " It's Mr. Justice Muttusammy Haiyar delivering judgment." When Wright passed the room about an hour later, the voice was still to be heard, and he asked what was then up. He got the exasperated reply, " Oh, it's that there Muttusammy Haiyar still delivering judgment. But, Lord love you, sir, what can you hexpect when you 'as these black-a—d savages in the 'Igh Court ? "

SECTION I.

GANJAM

At the back of the Ganjam, Vizagapatam, and Gōdāvari districts lies a vast area of hill and jungle known as the Agency Tracts, an area administered on primitive lines by the three Collectors in their capacity as Agents. I myself was never in this region, which is notorious for fevers " fed," as an old report funnily puts it, " by the gross atmosphere and fat fogs of the country." Even Blackwater fever is to be found there as well as the deer known as Bārasingh and the wild buffalo, while man-eating tigers seem to be particularly voracious, one of them being credited with over eighty victims. Moreover, one of the rivers of this part gives harbourage to a remarkable monster known as the Âvudu, which possesses a red head and four feet in shape resembling those of a peacock, attains a length of a hundred yards and feeds indiscriminately on cattle and elephants. The office work is or was a negligible quantity, insomuch that, when an Assistant Agent wants a day's shooting, all and sundry have been known to be summoned to help in beating by the announcement, " The Sarkar does business to-day."

Disturbances are not infrequent in these wild tracts in parts of which the people habitually carry neatly made and murderous-looking axes or tangis which they are apt when excited to use too freely. Of general outbreaks, or fituris, the worst in the last half-century or so was the rising in the Rampa country of Godāvari, in the course of which one of the Civilians concerned lost his wits under the stress of affairs, shot a harmless individual, and had to be removed to a lunatic asylum. The Agents and their Assistants have power to arrest mischievous persons under a sort of *lettre de cachet*, known as an Agency Warrant. I have known one to be issued by an Assistant for the recapture of a deserting cook, but it was generally recognized that he had overstrained the prerogative. The Agents have also the powers of District and Sessions Judges, the whole administration of the country being designed for the governance of people in an early stage of development. The way in which these people are regarded by the inhabitants of the ordinary areas was illustrated during the trial of a case of dacoity by H., one of the Agents. He was assisted by Assessors belonging to the low country, and at the end of the trial asked the First Assessor for his opinion. This was given in the following terms : "I think, your Honour, that there is no evidence that the accused are guilty, but, as they are Agency people, they may be convicted."

Ganjam and its Agency, or Māliah, tracts are associated in my mind with Tredegar, who, beginning life as a merchant, passed into the Police and spent many years at Bālligudda. He was riding one day through his wild domain when, to his vast surprise, he was accosted in French by an old man issuing from a hut. The language-puzzle was soon explained. The old man had been chosen as a boy to be a Meriah sacrifice, but had been rescued and taken to Europe as his servant by a military officer. In that capacity he spent many years in Paris, but there came upon him a yearning for the feverish hills and miserable hovels of his native land, and somehow or other he found his way back to them.

The Meriahs were human sacrifices offered by the Khonds to the Earth-goddess. The youths selected for the purpose, after being sumptuously treated for a year or so, were, when their time came, tied to a log, shaped roughly at one end like an elephant's head, which revolved upon an upright post. The tribesmen formed a circle, the log was swung round, and, as it passed them, the onlookers slashed strips of flesh off the miserable wretch with their knives ; then hurried away to bury the bloody fragments in their fields to ensure fertility. This abominable practice was suppressed in the 'thirties or 'forties, but in my own time, during a period of scarcity, the Government received a petition from a number of Khonds in which they prayed that, as a special favour, one human sacrifice might be allowed to them that year.

Another echo of past savagery came to me from Ganjam through a Sessions case. There was a temple of Kāli, and attached thereto a priest who brooded over the decay of faith. At last he unburdened his mind to a friend, a goldsmith, to whom he pointed out how bad season followed bad season and epidemic epidemic as a consequence of the unsatisfied thirst of Kāli for human blood. He then brought the conversation round to a certain carpenter, an enemy of the goldsmith, and suggested that, if this person could be enticed into the temple and slain there, the goddess would be propitiated and the world would be the better for the departure of an evil man. This proposition commended itself to the goldsmith, and it was arranged that he should seek reconciliation and, after sealing the truce by a liberal supply of liquor, lead the carpenter to his doom. To a certain point the plot succeeded, for the carpenter proved placable and accepted refreshment readily, but Fate ironically decreed that the carpenter should possess the stronger head and, by the time that a visit to the temple was mooted, he was by far the more sober. In fact, when the pair arrived at the shrine, the goldsmith was so drunk that, on prostrating himself before the idol, he was unable to get up again. The priest, whose detachment of mind and quickness of decision compel respect, grasped the position and its possibilities at once. He hurriedly expounded to the carpenter what religion and personal interest demanded of him and, meeting with a ready acceptance of his views, the enthusiastic minister of Kāli struck off the head of the goldsmith as he lay grunting before the altar.

The existence of a lingering belief in the efficacy of human sacrifice was indicated again at a time when a comet had sailed into view. I suppose it must have disturbed some people's minds, for a certain Sādhu, or ascetic, came into the Court of one of the Presidency Magistrates, declared that the apparition foreboded grave disasters to the people and the Government, and in the noblest manner besought the Magistrate to arrange that he should be offered up as a sacrifice to avert the impending afflictions.

Tredegar was the only man I have known who saw an elephant which had gone must, or masth, run amuck. The beast made a general onslaught upon a small village, and it was an extraordinary spectacle to see it going through the little houses as if they were made of cardboard and the people swarming out like ants. After raging about for a while, overturning and trampling underfoot, the elephant plunged down into the village tank. The Police then lined up along the walls of the tank and fired volleys until the maniac sank down.

My friend had various other experiences. He was sleeping one night upon straw when he woke up feeling something on his leg. He tried sleepily to brush it off with his other foot and received a sharp bite. Starting up, he saw by the light of the lamp the tail of a snake vanish under the kanāt of the tent and blood upon his leg. The butler had the reputation of being wise in snake-lore, and was sharply summoned. The question whether the bite was that of a venomous snake being urgently put, the butler examined the wound with intolerable deliberation before he replied, " I am not sure, but if Master begins to foam at the mouth, I shall know." On these words Tredegar foamed copiously, but nothing more happened in the course of the next agonizing hour or so.

Another time Tredegar had MacDonell as his companion in camp. They had separate sleeping-pāls, between which stood the tent for common use which contained the guns. Tredegar was awakened by a loud sniff at the foot of the kanāt, and his heart stood still. A few seconds later a tiger slouched slowly past the open door of the tent. Probably the light in the tent daunted it, for it moved off and made its presence in other parts of the encampment known by the scuffling of horses and trumpeting of elephants. Tredegar took advantage of the respite to dash across to the other tent. "MacDonell, MacDonell, there's a tiger in the camp." "Rot," replied MacDonell, awaking. He was answered from just without the tent by a long, threatening growl. MacDonell swung up on his haunches and the sweat sprang out on his face. In this case, too, the matter ended with the alarm, for, although the tiger roamed about the encampment all night and kept all on the alert, it did no more. Next morning, when the tents were struck, it reappeared and, by following the cavalcade for some distance, stimulated the rear-guard to give no cause of complaint for loitering.

Tredegar and Manning arranged a beat for bears and asked a little man called Jubb, an assistant in a merchant's office on the coast, to join them in camp for it. Jubb was posted in the middle and the beat began. Anon a deep "woof-woof" was heard, and the noise was repeated again and again with continuous, alternate rise and fall in the volume of sound. Tredegar could not imagine what was going on. As soon as the appearance of the beaters showed that the drive was over, Tredegar and Manning closed in upon Jubb. Him they found on his back, his face purple, his mouth open. What had happened was this. A she-bear with cubs had been started and she had come up against Jubb and gone for him. To and fro rushed the distracted little man with the bear at his heels. When the bear's teeth were just closing on him, he gained a respite by swinging round a tree and sprinting back again. So they kept at it, ding-dong, till the worried mother gave up the pursuit. A proposal for a second beat fell on deaf ears. Jubb returned to the camp, collected his effects, and made his way back to the coast.

Of man-hunting, also, Tredegar had some experience, for he was employed in suppressing the Rampa rebellion and also carried his police over the frontier to help in putting down a later rising on the part of Khonds in the Central Provinces. In the camp which he then joined, there were two ladies and a child. The camp was beleaguered, and one night the alarm spread that an attack was impending. Tredegar's movements were impeded by two night-gowned women who clung to him, but fortunately there was no onslaught to repel, and the outbreak was soon got under with the aid of measures of more severity than Tredegar considered to be necessary.

I heard a story of telepathy which concerns this very good friend of mine. At a time when, invalided on account of dysentery, he was on his way to his wife in England, she was sitting one day reading. Before her eyes the familiar surroundings changed suddenly into a scene at sea. She heard some one pronounce the words relating to committal of the body to the deep, saw a corpse dropped over the side of a ship, and noticed the splash which followed. Then the room regained its wonted look. In much agitation she telegraphed to Port Said for news and, after receiving a reassuring answer, wrote an account, to meet her husband at Marseilles, of what she had seen. When Tredegar got home he told his wife that, at the time when her vision occurred, a funeral was really in progress on his boat. A lady had died of dysentery and the service was held just by the deck-cabin where he was lying in the grip of the same disease. In much depression of mind he followed sentences which might soon be read over himself, and the words and the sound which his wife seemed to hear struck on his senses with particular force.

In the ugly house occupied by the Collector at Chatrapur I have spent some pleasant days. The programme of events was simple. Chhōta hāziri in the freshness to the strains of the usual crow-and-squirrel band, a strolling inspection in the fields, a comforting bath, enough papers to occupy the hot hours, three setts of tennis, an hour or two of Bridge, and perhaps a couple more men in to dinner ; these things, amid the informality of a bachelor establishment and in the entertaining society of McCrirrick, filled the time very agreeably.

Sometimes the routine was broken by an excursion. Thus McCrirrick and I went out for a night to a knot of stony hills some ten miles off after bears and, hearing on arrival that some had been seen, we sallied forth and traced a bear to a cave. McCrirrick got a shot through a cleft and out came the bear yelling and flung off helter-skelter down the hill pursued by ineffective bullets. We followed it to another cave, whence we had not dislodged it when darkness fell. Next morning we located a bear in a cave on the other side of the hill. A shikāri boldly entered and the animal retreated into an inner recess separated from the first by an opening to the air. Down the opening a man scrambled, only to return with monkey-like agility at the sound of a growl. Then the bear appeared and I shot it from above. Its groans went to my heart. We found it to be the animal wounded the previous day, and, considering the nature of the wound, it was amazing that the poor creature should have survived so long, and should have had strength to cross the ridge. One rarely hears of Europeans being injured by bears, but I knew one who had a mouthful which, fortunately, he could well spare taken out of his buttock, and heard of another being so badly bitten in the face that a part of the cheek-bone had to be removed.

Again I went with McCrirrick to Rambha, passing through the dreary, water-logged tract in which lie the remains of Old Ganjam, which was once the head-quarters of the district, but was abandoned on account of outbreaks of virulent fever. We stayed in a house belonging to the Raja of Kallikōta on the brim of the Chilka Lake, a large, shallow lagoon shut off from the sea, for the most part, by a strip of high land. On the lake great bags of duck and teal are made, and prawn-catching is carried on there on a large scale. The house at Rambha was comfortable enough, and actually possessed electric lights and a piped water supply, but it was choked with European furniture and the knick-knacks which Zamindars love to collect. From it we went to Kallikōta on the northernmost boundary of the Presidency, and found there a temple with the high curvilinear "sikra," which distinguishes the Northern Indian style. Inspection of this building showed that obscenity of adornment is not restricted to the Dravidian Vaishnavaite temple. The return to Rambha was effected by motor-car, canoe, and motor-launch, which last carried us for an hour or so on the pretty lake, passing several eyots covered with vegetation, on one of which is a bungalow built by a former Zamindar and in favour with honeymooning couples.

In the lake near Rambha is a little edifice which rises abruptly from the surface and is presumably built on a sunken rock. It is said to have been constructed by the old Collector Snodgrass that he might do his work there in peace and coolness and, one may fairly add, in secrecy. It is certainly not big enough to contain the mass of a modern Collector's daily correspondence, and perhaps Snodgrass resorted to it only to meditate on his sins. Tradition runs that, on rumours of his corruptness, the Government sent a Commissioner to make enquiries, and that, to frustrate these, Snodgrass threw the incriminating records into the lake. In the upshot he was, nevertheless, dismissed, and, the tale continues, made his way to London, where he took a crossing opposite the building occupied by the Court of Directors. Here, besom in hand, he stood humbly touching his hat to old acquaintances until the nuisance grew unbearable. So the Court voted him a pension, and the following day, being in fact in affluent circumstances all the while, he drove up in a coach and four to tender his thanks to that body.

There was another old Collector of Ganjam whose renown, an honourable renown, long lingered in the district, and C., when Assistant Collector, was greatly interested to learn that there still lived an old man who had known him. C. sent for this patriarch and began to question him eagerly. " Is it true that you once saw Mr. —— ? " " It is true." " And did he speak to you ? " " He did." " What did he say to you ? " " He said," the old man answered with simple pride, "Pō bāhinchūt " (" Get away, you —— "). Strange that this light, familiar greeting should have lain embalmed for half a century in the aged man's heart and perfumed, as one may say, his whole life.

There is another building in Ganjam which is attributed to Snodgrass who, at least, left his mark on the district. It used to be known far and wide as " The house at Aska." I never saw it ; from accounts it was a palatial dwelling, " bright with porphyry and syenite." It passed into the hands of a man whose hospitality became famous, and it was whispered that the domestic service therein was, on occasions of high festival, rendered by damsels who did not possess even that ultimate garment which the poet reserves for Lady Godiva. In the house stood two life-sized, wooden figures of women. It chanced that Colonel Campbell came to stay there at a time when some young men also were being entertained as guests, and a tent for his use was pitched in the compound. Colonel Campbell was well known as a man of sage conduct and sober conversation. Actuated by no ignoble motive, but by a desire to give their senior an opportunity to demonstrate the strength of his principles, those young men took one of the aforesaid figures and, towards eventide, laid it reverently in the Colonel's bed, covering it with a sheet. Ten o'clock came and the young men, feigning weariness, went off to hold vigil by the tent. A quarter of an hour later Colonel Campbell bade good night to his host. He crossed the compound at a slow pace, calling loudly as he went, "Boy, Boy." "Sah," answered a distant voice. The servant hastened; the officer entered the tent. Instantly he reappeared outside and in hurried but kindly accents cried out, "All right, Boy. I shan't want you to-night. You can go back to bed."

Section 2

VIZAGAPATAM

A great and noble district of which I know little more than could be gained from a few visits to Waltair, lying up against the high headland known as the Dolphin's Nose, which forms a striking contrast to the general flatness of the Madras coast, and has earned notoriety for malaria, albeit, to appearance, healthy as Beachy Head. My host on the occasion of one of my visits, the Collector of the time being, was a sufferer from asthma and displayed a curious intolerance of horses. A ride, or even a drive in a carriage, would be followed by a period of prostration in bed. This officer was appointed executor under the will of a wealthy Zamindarni in the Vizagapatam district and, on her death, went to her house to take charge of the property. He found that the lady had been in occupation of six rooms and in all these the floors were heaped with an extraordinary collection of clothes, toys, jewellery, knick-knacks, and rubbish of all sorts. A common little box lying on the floor of one of the rooms was found to contain one hundred and thirty currency notes for R.10,000 each and, altogether, about fifteen lakhs' worth of personal property was discovered. I knew another Collector of the district of whom it was reported that a singular accident interposed between him and sudden death. It fell to his lot to follow up a wounded tigress, and a premonition of evil induced him to make his will before doing so. Chance robbed the message of its value. The tigress did indeed charge the sportsman, but in her rush she was caught round the neck by a creeper and brought to a momentary halt which sealed her doom. I have heard it said that a tiger will never charge home if its pursuer stands rigidly motionless ; it will always swerve when a yard or two off. This seems probable enough, but I never met anyone who had tried the experiment.

Lack of other material induces me to fill up this section with some references to Drake-Ballater, whom I associate mainly with Vizagapatam as I do Tredegar with Ganjam. Drake-Ballater was a tall, good-looking man who never tired in discoursing upon the high lineage and hereditary comeliness of his family. I met him first at a dinner-party which proved a dreary affair, for D.-B. stifled conversation at table by a lecture on his staple topic, and the rest of the evening up to a late hour was devoted by Tibbit and me to a vain attempt to outsit him. This was done at the request of our hostess, who was afraid of being left alone with that reputedly ardent gentleman. I next heard of D.-B. at Liverpool. My cousin, returning home one evening, told me that, whilst he was having lunch at a restaurant, there had entered a man who, after a glance round, had announced loudly his intention to stand champagne to all present. This offer not having evoked an effusive response, the stranger fell into a state of anger, and reproached the company with its lack of appreciation of the condescension of one who in India had life and death in his hands. I had no difficulty in identifying the stranger. I think that I next heard of him as appearing in a London Police Court to explain why he was wandering about with a woman dressed as a boy. I do not recollect why the police had interfered, but I remember D.-B.'s explanation to have been that he was trying, through his companion, to spread Mr. Joseph Chamberlain's political views among the working classes and that the disguise was useful for this purpose. He was, I think, discharged with a caution or something of that sort. He came into the light again in connection with the mutiny of a sepoy regiment. On this occasion he, as District Magistrate, made to the Government the suggestion, practical if unusual, that the mutineers should be brought to a proper sense of subordination by being driven on board a brig at anchor in the surf with a view to their experiencing sea-sickness in its most violent form. He was at home not long afterwards, and on his return voyage caused amusement by a letter written to a fellow-passenger whom he reproached for want of respect towards one possessing power over life and death, and, in order that the recipient of the letter might appreciate the danger of arousing his anger, he cited the case of a Vakīl who, having offended him in Court and having received as a consequence the full blast of his wrath, fell down insensible and lay in a swoon for a long while. Back again in India, he soon, as might be expected, caused scandal by further eccentricities. For example, the Government received a complaint against him written by a Vakīl who had reason to demur to the treatment accorded to him on the occasion of a call. The memorialist began by describing his visit, and his friendly talk with the Judge. It was when the Vakīl rose from his seat, in response to the customary hint, that D.-B. departed from the usual formalities of farewell. What happened then can best be described in the words of the petition: "He shook me by the hand, and, saying in a mocking way, 'Well, good-bye, old fellow,' kicked me down the stairs."

As a result of such matters D.-B. was summoned to Madras for an inquiry into the state of his mind. Arrived there, he visited a horse-dealer, from whom he ordered some fifty animals. His object in making such an extensive purchase was, as he explained, to have all these animals paraded, in jhools bearing his initials, in front of Government House, and by this means to impress the Governor with a sense of the social importance of the man whose case was under consideration.

It need hardly be said that the medical opinion on the case resulted in D.-B.'s removal from the active list, but I caught one or two more glimpses of him.

Once in a letter to a newspaper. In this he enlarged upon his favourite subject, the Drake-Ballater family, and mentioned that he had observed the same favourable physical type in a princely stock in India and also in the neighbourhood of Boulogne. This remark was followed immediately by the words : "I had an uncle who lived for a long time at Boulogne. There may be more in this than meets the eye." Again in a puff of a hair restorer. Therein appeared his likeness with a letter asserting that he had been bald, or nearly so, before using the wash to which was to be ascribed the thick crop of curly hair visible in the photograph. As a fact he was all his life the possessor of a fine head of hair.

Section 3

KISTNA

Largely a monotonous rice-flat, Kistna is notorious officially for the inordinate amount of work which it supplies to the Collector and universally for intolerable heat. There was a day in the month of May some years ago which has become locally historical on account of the temperature reached. That day White was engaged on the Divi pumping-works. Thirteen of the coolies employed there under him died of sunstroke, crows dropped dead out of the trees, his dog was kept alive by wrapping it in a grass-mat over which water trickled continuously. The night was almost as dreadful as the day. White shared a tent with another man. They kept a lamp burning between the beds so that each might be able to detect on the other's face the first symptoms of trouble, for they hardly expected to get safely through those suffocating hours.

The backlands of the district supply some big-game shooting. I think it was there that Cholmondeley of the Civil Service had his uncomfortable night with a tiger. There had been a kill, and Cholmondeley took his station close by, on the ground, behind some bushes. In the early part of his vigil he was entertained by the antics of smaller animals round the body. First appeared a jackal, which trotted casually past the kill, making an obvious pretence not to see it. Then it re-passed at a gallop. Appearing again, it stole cautiously up to the carcass, leapt back, and rushed away. Finding that these tricks had not brought any dangerous enemy upon the scene, the cunning beast returned and began to feed, and, while it fed, a swarm of other jackals which now came into view circled round it in constant movement. The first one having sated its appetite, another took its place, while the throng continued its gyration. Suddenly all fled, and a hyæna slouched up and started to feed, but it ate in evident fear, for, after each mouthful, it glanced round apprehensively. Then it too vanished, and a tiger, enormous in the moonlight, stalked forward. Cholmondeley fired, and there burst forth a most hideous din of yells and roars. On this, the man carrying the second rifle made off at his best pace, and so appalling was the outcry that Cholmondeley was afraid by firing again to make his whereabouts known to the tiger, which was writhing and crawling within half a dozen yards of him. So there he lay, fearful of moving a limb, and ardently desirous of a change of scene. Gradually the noise died down, and when dawn came it was found that the wounded animal had dragged itself away, nor was it seen again.

Kay's plan of shooting over a kill was different. He would spread a mattress by the body, put a fence round the mattress, and set up a pole bearing an electric light. As soon as he heard the sound of feeding, he switched on the light and fired. Often, he said, he had tigers and panthers so near him that he could have touched them, but they never seemed to be aware of his presence, so defective is their sense of smell.

I have no intimate knowledge of the district, but have been on the fine canal which conveys the Gōdāvari water by a thousand arteries to the paddy-fields, and visited Ellore and Masulipatam. A glimpse at this last place reveals broad roads bordered with strips of grass and trees, and a town dying apathetically of inanition as a result of the silting up of the sea. Years ago, in 1864 to be precise, there arose in the Bay of Bengal a swelling pregnant with disaster to Masulipatam. The monstrous wave moved resistlessly through the little old fort, covered the low ground beyond, trampled the town underfoot, and pressed with solemn power over the flat country-side. Seventeen miles inland marched the great flood, and, retiring, it left the ground littered with the bodies of thousands of men and animals. An eye-witness of the catastrophe described it to me.

In the fort I have just alluded to there is a small church built by a General Pator (I think that is the name) in memory of his mistress Arabella Robinson. The story, as I remember it, is that burial in consecrated ground was refused, and so the bereaved man constructed a church to enclose her tomb. The body is said to have been embalmed and placed in a glass case over which slid a marble slab, but some person, whether because he grudged the immortality bestowed upon the features of a sinful woman or because the body had become an unseemly sight, cemented the slab permanently over the case.

The sceptre once held by Masulipatam has

passed to Bēzwāda, where, a prey to sand-flies, I once spent some weeks. The town chokes in the clutch of arid hills which end in a bluff up against the broad Kistna river at the point of radiation of the canals for the irrigation of two deltas. In the middle of the town rises a rocky hillock bearing a couple of small houses, in one of which an English lady died of heat-apoplexy on the May day already mentioned. Scrambling one morning over this eminence, I almost fell over a bear. On recovery from the stupefaction caused by encountering such an animal in such a place, I made off in search of a rifle. I returned with a companion, both of us armed to the teeth. We selected one of the bungalows as the point from which we should work the hill, climbed up to it, and found the bear tied up in the verandah. It proved to be the property of a man who was passing through the place. At the foot of this hillock is a humble structure which forms the Freemasons' Lodge. I have seen it stated that such Lodges are often known among the people as Headcutting Houses. This may be so, and perhaps in public estimation they are associated with unholy rites. Anyway, some years ago, the Acting Governor of Madras who was a Mason attended a ceremony at this particular house and departed. Soon afterwards an excited mob of some five hundred persons armed with sticks gathered together and began to make a disturbance. They were dispersed with some difficulty as they were firmly persuaded that the high functionary in question had been occupied at the Lodge in offering up a human sacrifice.

Opposite Bēzwāda, across the river, at Ūndavalli, there is a cave-temple excavated in the side of a hill. The cave, which is probably artificial in part, is provided (one can hardly say adorned) with pillars and figures, and is arranged to form a temple of four floors connected, as regards three of them, by steps. I have not seen elsewhere anything of quite the same sort. The workmanship which is of the roughest is generally attributed to the Pallavas and the sixth or seventh century.

Kondapalli is reached by a short railway journey from Bēzwāda. It is well known as a place where a score or so of families manufacture out of "pōliki" wood small figures known as Kondapalli toys, purely trivial articles which tourists buy for some reason or other. The village is rotten with fever, and the inhabitants are miserably poor. A walk of forty minutes up rugged, overgrown hills which reach perhaps 1500 feet at the summits brings one to a ridge and to a gateway in the innermost of two walls which embrace part of the miniature range. At that point there opens out a view of rocky peaks, a large pool, much growth of tree and bush, high walls extending over a considerable area, and the remnants of a palace of which there exist intact only some big vaults, and a corner which is used as a sort of Travellers' bungalow. The evening light flooded the scene with gold and struck a green sparkle from the parrots as they whizzed across with piercing shrieks.

Many chieftains, Reddis, Gajapatis, Mussalmāns, have made their eyry behind the ramparts which still weave their complicated pattern over the hillsides. At the foot of the hills is one of those little graveyards, more than sufficiently abundant in India, in which the dreams of youth have ended. For they are dedicated mainly to the young; subalterns and corporals and privates; the prey of Battle and Disease; humble and forgotten workers upon the vast, frail edifice of Empire.

Section 4

KURNOOL

The backbone of the inland district of Kurnool is the wooded, malarious range known as the Nallamalais, where dwell the Chentsus who take their simple pleasures in the form of fights, murders, and drinking bouts. These primitive people still use bows and arrows, and quite recently a Superintendent of Police, who went with a *posse* into the hills to round up an offender, was received with a shower of arrows, one of which went through his topi. A grateful folk, too; they deified Tibbit, who had a lot to do with them, and, on his departure, put up in his honour a shrine at which suitable oblations were offered. I do not know whether this is still done. Very likely it is. For many years a lonely European tomb in the Tinnevelly district was laden at appointed seasons by the people living around with gifts of alcohol and cheroots.

European officers usually like Kurnool. I do not know why, for a more dreary and forbidding country I have rarely seen. Also it is for the most part feverish. Round Kurnool Town—a withered hag, in the tatters of outworn finery, crouching on the bank of the Tungabhadra—the scenery is particularly morose, a black desolation when the crops are off the ground. The town itself is worthy of some attention. The view of the old walls from the river is not without charm, and there are crumbling ruins which speak of better days. One of these contains some good stucco window-tracery, and the place possesses the best Muhammadan tomb of the Presidency, that of Abdul Wahāb. This does not mean that the building is comparable with such grave and stately edifices as the tomb of Humāyūn at Delhi, but it is worth seeing, and the dome is said to be composed of a single, hollowed stone. In the river a high, spindle-shaped, stone structure formed, as they say, the basement of a pleasure-house of the Nawābs of Kurnool, whose possessions were annexed in or about the 'thirties.

A smaller river on the other side of the town, the Hendri, is notorious for the floods which it brings down. When Stark was Collector the water rose nine or ten feet above the ground-level of his house, and he had quite an exciting night of it. While I stayed with him he regaled me with accounts of his adventures on that occasion and of experiences in the North of India. One of these latter, a ridiculous little story, sticks in my memory. At some Viceregal function or other, at which there was a terrible crush, his eye was drawn to a little Bengali Bābu who was wedged tightly between two stalwart military officers bristling with hard points, sword-hilts, spurs, elbows, and so on. The pressure increased, and, when it reached its highest point, the little Bābu bleated protestingly, "Please, I am about to vomit." It was fine to see the martial promptitude and decision with which those two warriors thereupon clove themselves a way through the palpitating mass.

When the railway-line was first opened in the district, W. passed over it on a pilot engine. He told me that numbers of women ran to the side of the line on that occasion, and awaited the approaching engine with uplifted cloths. It was supposed that these were persons afflicted with barrenness who expected fecundation by the rushing power of the locomotive.

There is a small Native State, Banganapalli, which is supervised by the Collector of Kurnool in the capacity of Political Agent. At one time, during a minority, the State was under the management of a Civilian, O'Connell, who, visiting the jail of the place, found some prisoners who had got into it in a rather unusual way. It seems that some years before a civil suit had been instituted before the Dewān, who came to the, doubtless correct, conclusion that both the parties and all the witnesses were lying. So without more ado he there and then clapped the whole lot into prison with instructions that they should remain there for periods ranging up to seven years. This must have had a most discouraging effect upon Civil litigation. It was part of O'Connell's duty to introduce a system of local self-government into the State. It may surprise some to learn that this reform was not universally welcomed, and an old Mussalmān probably voiced general opinion when he condemned the change in an indignant conversation with O'Connell. "Are you not paid to govern us?" "Well, yes, I am." "Then why do you trouble us by asking us to help you?"

Section 5

ANANTAPUR

The capital town, of the same name, is a nice enough little place with a cheerful appearance of adolescence. It is the centre of the Munro tradition, for it is here that that great man had his headquarters when he ruled as Principal Collector the wide realm of the Ceded Districts. His house still stands, but it is so mean an abode for so important a personage that local legend represents it as merely his seraglio. The most interesting places in the district are, however, Gooty and Penukonda. The former boasts a hill-fort which (Gingee, which I have not seen, excepted) may be regarded as the most noteworthy in Madras.

The hill lifts itself a thousand feet into the sunshine, and over its ridges and dips the ancient wall rises and falls until it drops to a gateway in the midst of a crowd of those small, flat-roofed, stone houses which compose the villages of the Ceded Districts. Where the citadel crowns the gigantic rock which forms the summit is a set of cells where prisoners were hidden away in darkness preparatory, as tradition goes, to being sent flying over a cliff for the entertainment of the genial Marātha chieftain, Morāri Rāo. I was accompanied to the top by a forward, English-speaking Brahman, who emphasized his presence by incessant chatter and by a howl of affected alarm whenever I slipped on the smooth-worn path. This person was a wanderer who spent his time roaming from place to place in search of a job. He never, apparently, found one and, when the poor fellow felt what he termed "belly-pinch" at one place, he moved on to another.

Sir Thomas Munro's body lay for some time at Gooty (it was afterwards taken to Madras), and the memory of him fills the place. There is also a memorial to one Hampana, whose death at the hands of English soldiers created strong feeling a quarter of a century or so ago. I was present in the High Court when the charge against these men came on for trial. The story of the prosecution was that Hampana was killed while defending a woman against outrage, but the case ended in an acquittal.

Penukonda is the place to which the stricken Vijayanagar dynasty betook itself after the fatal battle of Tālikōta in the sixteenth century. On the way to the spot from Anantapur one passes, when still some miles off, between barren hillocks, which with their dun flanks and high black spines, resemble monstrous, crouching dragons. The ill-built, crowded little town contains many Muhammadans who have an air of desperate poverty. It is ringed round with stony fells the highest of which carries some ruins of no consequence, and there is a profusion of shattered buildings and defensive walls. Nothing has any architectural merit, but there are a few things which deserve a hasty visit. For instance, there is the Moslemized Hindu temple called Bāpayya's tomb, through the roof of which grows a tree strange to the townsfolk as to myself. It is known as the Sugar tree because of the quality of the sap. There is also a mosque within two of the pillars of which are small, carved, revolving columns—a curious freak of fancy. Finally, there is the Gāgana Mahāl, which is the palace, or part of the palace, wherein the reduced and impoverished rulers took refuge. It looks well from a distance, and is an interesting relic of civil architecture, but it is of poor workmanship and cramped dimensions.

Shortly before my visit there was an outbreak of plague at Penukonda. One of the victims was a monkey, and, on its death, its companions would not allow any human being to approach the carcass. In the end they carried it away and deserted the town in a body. I give the above on the authority of the Indian Collector of the district. He had formerly been a Deputy Collector under me, and did well in rising to the position of Collector, but another of my Deputies, soared higher still by establishing a claim to a peerage.

Section 6

CHITTOOR

Following the trail of the wounded and expiring Vijayanagar Monarchy, one passes into the favoured district of Chittoor, which was carved, not long ago, out of the districts of North Arcot and Cuddapah. Half of it is a high tableland which produces in particular profusion that yellow-flowered cassia bush, known as tangedu or āvaram, which, for some obscure reason, no caste-man may cut. The other half is an engaging combination of fell and flat.

On the plateau stands Madanapalli, which has already been referred to, and Punganūr, where the Zamindar accommodates European travellers in a small house distinguished by a verandah-balustrade composed of empty beer-bottles. It stands in a garden which is said to have been designed by that cunning Civilian-gardener Wrigley, who set up the stone bearing lines from Pindar which surprises the passing traveller at Palmanēr. That officer is my authority for saying that, once upon a time, the Board of Revenue possessed a Secretary named Jackson who, being of an aggressive disposition while the Members whom he served sought only for tranquillity, gradually drew all power into his own hands. In the end he was issuing orders freely of his own authority, although, in cases of exceptional importance, he sent these to the Members "for perusal" after issue. In course of time there came upon the scene a new Member of less retiring character, and a quarrel between him and the masterful Secretary was attended by such insubordination on the part of the latter that the Government, with some sharp comments, transferred him to the post of Divisional Officer in Kurnool. Indignant at this treatment, Jackson declined to do any work, and, on the Collector's complaint, a Member of the Board went down to investigate. He found in Jackson's office piles of unopened covers, and reported the fact to the Government. Called upon to answer the charge, Jackson declined to furnish any explanation until the Government had withdrawn the remarks they had made about his conduct as Secretary. On this he was reduced to the post of Assistant Collector, and in that position he remained for several years. Then Lord Napier came out as Governor, and, finding a comparatively senior officer kicking his heels as Assistant Collector, made some inquiry into his case and gazetted him to act as Collector of Kistna. Of this order of transfer and promotion Jackson took no manner of notice, and, when called on to explain, he replied that, until the Government withdrew their previous obnoxious remarks, he must decline to recognize their existence or the validity of any orders issued by them. This was too much, and Jackson was removed from the service by the Secretary of State.

When I reached Punganūr with my wife and the Collector, the Raja asked us to dine at his house. It is not to be understood that we were asked to dine *with* him. The dinner was cooked and served by our own servants, and we and the Collector dined alone. It is only in India that such a form of hospitality would be conceivable. The host did, however, supply some of the dishes, notably a good curry, the main constituent of which was a confection of wheat tasting much like meat. Before dinner we had seen over part of the Raja's house. It contains a museum instituted by a former Zamindar. The principal feature of this is a set of almost life-size figures, representing people of various castes, made of plaster and coloured. These figures, some of which are very good, were made on the spot and certain of them by the former Raja himself. There is also in the house a handsome throne covered with silver plates. This is said to have been presented to the family in its original wooden form by the Emperor Akhbār, and to have been overlaid with the metal afterwards.

The town of Chittoor is a pretty place of rocky

hillocks, trees, and bushes. Its well-wooded appearance may be partly due to Wrigley, who employed one of his Assistants on going to and fro in stony places and dropping seeds in likely spots. The place is wild enough to produce an occasional panther, and one of these animals has been known to sit on the hill above the Vakīls' tennis-court watching the play.

While staying at Chittoor, I was told of a faction feud which had some unusual features. Faction A., by judicious arrangements, had got a member of Faction B. into jail. The next move was to B., and they sent for a famous Yōgi to do a little blasting on A. He demanded fifty rupees for the job. This was felt to be profiteering in magic, and B. demurred to paying so much until, at all events, the Yōgi had given a satisfactory sample of his power. Thereupon the Yōgi pointed to a flourishing tree and declared that on the following day it would be found to be withered and dead. So, indeed, it befell, and the bargain was struck. Then things began to happen. A member of A. died suddenly. This was gratifying, and, when other deaths followed in quick succession in A., the members of B. felt that they had laid out their money on a really first-class line of witchcraft. Afterwards, however, deaths began to occur outside the circle of A., and it turned out that pneumonic plague had settled on the village. Such dangers have to be faced by those who dabble in the Black Art, and the visitation does not seem to have affected the reputation of the sorcerer. In fact, the surviving villagers were at the time proudly showing the withered tree as a proof of his professional ability.

When the luckless representatives of the kingly house of Vijayanagar left Penukonda under imperious pressure, they migrated to Chandragiri, where, alongside a knife-edge of rock, they built them a palace and a fortress. The latter is of rough and hasty workmanship. Of the former there remain the dwellings of the king and his consorts. They are of several storeys, and of rather remarkable shape, owing to their extreme shallowness among other things. The accommodation provided in them is scanty, and they arouse little interest except as good specimens of the elder Dravidian domestic architecture of which few examples survive. I have seen the remains of the Vijayanagar dynasty's buildings at all its three capitals, and they left on my mind the impression, not to be removed by glowing descriptions on the part of some contemporary writers, that, notwithstanding the extensiveness of their dominions, these rulers maintained little state and dwelt in comparatively humble surroundings. It was from Chandragiri that issued the fateful decree assigning to the English Company the site of Fort St. George.

From that place I made a shooting excursion with the Sub-Collector and his wife. I remember that we started on Good Friday, because a native gentleman concluded a visit to us on the previous evening by the polite wish that we should all enjoy "a happy Good Friday." We camped at Nāgapatla at the head of the Chāmila Valley, which cuts for ten miles or so into that tangle of hills which includes the sacred mount of Tirumalai. The valley is reported to swarm with tigers, and Hatfield came there upon a space of open ground which looked like a shambles, for within a few square yards lay the remains of four fine sambhur stags which had been killed by tigers. Further, the local tigers are reputed to be of such formidable strength that they can snap an elephant chain. An explanation of this saying occurred to me when I found that the buffaloes tied beneath our machāns were indeed tethered by chains, but that these chains were attached to their necks by thin cords.

We stayed several days in our camp, and R. and I duly sat for hours in our machāns but no four-footed beast came near us. Perhaps the presence of wild-dogs accounted for this, the deer disappearing before them and, on the track of the deer, their feline foes. From my machān I got capital views of that charming bird the Paradise flycatcher which abounds in these woods. The cock has two very long tail-feathers, which are white in the adult, chestnut in the young. Attention is quite likely to be first drawn to the bird by the surprising spectacle of a white satin ribbon rippling, apparently of its own volition, through the foliage of a tree, the black body not being discernible. Whilst I was watching these birds dipping into a pool and listening intently for the stealthy footfalls which never came, the air was quivering to an oft-repeated sound, a long-drawn, soft, sweet braying. This seems like a contradiction in terms, but those who know the cry of the pretty little cock-Iora will understand what I mean.

The result of the expedition was a peahen and a miss at a Spotted stag.

In the company of the same young couple I paid a visit to Kālahasti. We put up in a building which was erected at the cost of a lakh of rupees by the then Zamindar for the purpose of housing for one or two days Lord Napier the Governor, and he never visited the place after all. The house contained the things usual in Zamindars' houses, but also a fine set of ivory chessmen of peculiar design. The town of Kālahasti was the headquarters of a chiefdom of power and renown, but the Zamindāri family has fallen upon evil days. I thought that I had never seen a more typically Indian picture when I first saw from beyond the river the huddle of irregular buildings and the temple backed by a rocky hill. This sanctuary is of high repute, and the festivals connected with it serve as a potent means of spreading cholera.

The purpose of my journey to Kālahasti was to attend a public meeting. When that was over, we were provided with an illustration of the growth of a corporate spirit among non-Brahmans as against the dominant class. We were conducted to a dingy courtyard in the middle of which was a raised, open pavilion. Therein we sat while a born orator poured forth a vigorous Telugu oration. At the conclusion of the speech, tea was served to us in our uncomfortably prominent position, while the less distinguished guests had the privilege of watching each morsel proceed to its destination. From this entertainment all Brahmans were excluded.

That night, very tired, I watched from a balcony the Sivarātri ceremony : the tossing, flaring torches, the sweating men staggering under the heavy vāhanams which bore the sacred images, the surging crowd. A suffocating darkness brooded over the scene.

Section 7

NORTH ARCOT

North Arcot is the parent by fission of Chittoor, in throwing off which it has lost a great deal, but enough is left for the district to be still regarded with favour. At Vellore, the headquarters, there is a remarkably pleasing specimen of Southern Indian military architecture. Around this fort is a moat, which is backed by a low wall with rounded battlements and semicircular bastions. The line of circumvallation is broken here and there by small towers continued downwards in ornamental fashion, the common and graceful representation of the drooping plantain-flower being most conspicuous. Agreeable to the eye of the casual visitor, these ornaments must have been still more so to persons contemplating an escalade. Behind this outer wall rise higher ramparts with openings for cannon and rounded bastions. The temple within the fort is not in use, and so can be seen in its entirety. A gopuram with a fine, lofty door opens on to a handsome cloister, at one corner of which stands a mantapam rising in stages to a central dais. The mantapam has numerous pillars, many of which are provided with a round pilaster in front after the fashion at once so common and so effective. The pillars generally are carved with remarkable finish. Within the cloister is a second, plainer one which surrounds the principal building wherein an ambulatory encompasses dark, windowless cells, the innermost of which once contained the image of Īsvara.

The only other place which I have visited in the district is Arcot. There is little left there to indicate its past importance and performances ; just a city-gate and a broad rampart alongside the river.

The district contains an unusually large proportion of Muhammadans, and, for that reason, religious disturbances are unusually rife there. At Arcot, at the time of the Mutiny, bigger things were threatened. The tale, as I remember it, runs that a Mussalmān raised the standard of revolt there, and, collecting some "badmāshes," marched about proclaiming his independent sovereignty. The District Magistrate, by name Brett, dealt with the situation with great discretion. Hurrying to the spot, he issued a summons to the new ruler. A considerable loss of reputation followed that potentate's compliance with the process, and his discomfiture was complete when the District Magistrate disposed of his pretensions by inflicting a fine of ten rupees for causing a public nuisance in the streets.

When I went out to India all the Muhammadans wore their national turban, the most dignified and picturesque of head-dresses. Now that is giving way, a change significant of the growth of a pan-Islamic sentiment, to the abominable fez, which lends to the face a peculiarly vulgar and debauched appearance.

Those who wish to know more about an interesting district, I must refer to the *District Gazetteer*, or to the older *District Manual* compiled by Loosemore, long Collector there. Loosemore had great facility with the pen, and much curious information and many striking observations appeared, I believe, in the original draft of his Manual. The propriety which distinguishes all Anglo-Saxon Administrations threw the Government of Madras into a cold sweat of fear over the manuscript, and they directed one of their Under Secretaries to eliminate all passages unsuitable for family reading. The young man worked hard, but *non semper arcum tendit Apollo* and, at times, overwhelmed with the magnitude of the task, the censor nodded, so that there remain in the published work oases of unexpected refreshment.

They say that, shortly before Loosemore's retirement, he sent in a frolicsome protest against his supersession for some appointment or other in these terms : "When Mr. A. superseded me, I did not, of course, protest as he was a brother-in-law of the Senior Member of Council, nor, similarly, in the case of Mr. B. who was related to the Junior Member. Mr. C., however, has no such special claim to advancement, and I feel bound to represent my case." This memorial was leniently regarded as a mere joke, and perhaps the story is little better.

Section 8

SALEM

Of this district also I have seen very little. It is principally famous for mangoes and the Salem Riots. It also possesses the hill-station of Yercaud, which stands on the plateau of the Shevaroys at an elevation of about 4,500 feet.

There is plenty of jungle on this mountain block, and it improves on the way up until, on the tableland, the vegetation is almost too rank. Flowers grow luxuriantly, especially plumbago, which forms high hedges, and shoe-flower or hibiscus, which produces blossoms almost as large as cheese-plates. There are shady ways for walking and a climate neither hot nor cold, but at times Yercaud is somewhat malarious. There is practically no game, but, in spite of the French priests who are charged with killing every small bird they see, the place is resonant at seasons with the cries of barbets.

One of the European houses on these hills deserves mention. It stands where Shevarāyan lifts his bald crown to the altitude of 5,400 feet, and is at the foot of a cliff in a grove of trees. To reach it an entrance has been cut through a big rock. A charming, though damp, dwelling for such as seek seclusion, and in England, in these houseless days, it makes the mouth water to remember that it was then offered for sale at 1200 rupees. There is at Ootacamund a house similarly remote from the main station. It was incautiously built beneath a great boulder, which, getting dislodged, crashed through the roof and filled most of the drawing-room ; notwithstanding this the house is still occupied. Mrs. B. used to live there. One night she was disturbed by hearing something moving about in a room. She got up and locked the door of the room, thinking that whatever was inside might as well stay there till the morning. Next day the inmates discovered that they had trapped a black panther, which they allowed to escape.

At the time of the Afrīdi campaign an extraordinary panic seized on the (Indian presumably) inhabitants of Yercaud. The rumour spread that the Afrīdis, with fine disregard of distance, were marching upon the place, and, to allay fear, the local volunteers were actually put under arms and spent a night at the head of the ghāt-road, which is the main means of access to the station. As an alternative to it, there is a short-cut of seven miles, which may be done in a canvas-chair slung on poles, but the track is so rough and steep that most prefer to walk. Those who use the chair will find that the bearers soothe their labours by a continuous chant. The men behind start with "Wokkong," to which those in front respond with "Tāyī"; this is followed from the rear by "Yogong," to which the answer is "Tarmā." The sounds uttered by the hind bearers seem to have no particular meaning which, I am sure, is much to the credit of those toiling men.

The mention of the Afrīdi scare reminds me that many years ago there spread among the residents of Ootacamund a rumour that, on a certain night, the Muhammadans would rise and massacre the Europeans. This was fully believed by, among others, Mrs. C., the wife of a Member of Council, and she arranged to have a dinner-party that night for men only. Nor did she confine her hospitality to bachelors, for a married man whom I met got an invitation, at the foot of which was noted "Please bring your gun." He went, too, leaving his wife to her fate.

Just one more paltry anecdote from Salem, and I am done with the district. When B. was District Magistrate there, a Vakīl appeared before him in camp at a late hour to present an application on behalf of an acrobat, who was charged with some offence or other. B. refused to hear the Vakīl then, but told him that, if he did not mind unconventional attire, he might appear before him next morning before he moved camp. So the Vakīl appeared, and argued his case before B., who sat under a tree looking as dignified as a suit of striped pyjamas permitted. A comic background to the scene was furnished by the other members of the acrobatic troupe who, to awaken B.'s interest and sympathy, stood on their heads or turned somersaults while the Vakīl was delivering his address.

Section 9

SOUTH ARCOT

One evening in Madras I was with my wife in the house when we heard a low moaning out at sea. The noise grew until " the blast of the Terrible Ones " was full upon us. I sprang to close the French windows and the panes were blown in, the electric light went out, and instantly the room was full of things that fought and clutched and screamed. Suddenly the room was empty again, and the Jinns were wailing in the distance, leaving peace behind them. The track of the storm was only about fifty yards in width. Tiles had been torn off the next house, young trees, of no tough sort indeed, had been shorn through as by a knife, others had been uprooted.

That was my only and inadequate experience of such hurricanes as, in the season of the north-east monsoon, smite the districts to which I am now leading the way. Some acquaintances of mine were on their way from Madras to Cuddalore, the chief town of South Arcot, when a gale of this sort leapt into being. So furious was the wind that the train was actually held up, and, after standing rocking on the rails for a bit, a part of it went quietly over on one side. I do not think that any of the passengers were injured, and they spent the night as best they could in the recumbent carriages. Another train, travelling in the reverse direction, was overturned at the same time, and the tempest reached such a pitch of fury that people were swept off their feet and struck dead against walls and trees.

In the European quarter of Cuddalore is peace, deep peace. For a few days the quietness of the forsaken roads and placid backwater, a tranquillity hardly stirred by the murmur of the surf and the rattling of the verandah-chicks in the sea-breeze, is vastly agreeable. I can, however, imagine that, in a short while, the leaden cope of lethargy becomes a torment, and I know few things more depressing than the dilapidated, half-lit, lone-standing bungalow which serves as a Club, where three or four men meet after sunset to play snookers and crack feeble jokes.

Evidence of more stirring times is afforded by the remains of a miniature stronghold, a work so small that it is with surprise one learns that it is the once well-known Fort St. David. A glance suffices for that relic, and another may be bestowed upon the old "Garden House," where the Collector lives. The extensive, low-ceilinged room on the ground floor has watched two centuries or so pass by, but the story that Clive occupied the building is discredited.

In the suburb called Tirupāpuliyūr is a temple conspicuous for its ill-mannered notice forbidding "Christians, Muhammadans, and lepers" from entering any portion of it, and in New Town one more honourably distinguished by the fine stonework done therein by the Nāttukkottai Chettis.

In the church in Old Town is a tablet in memory of C. E. Macdonald, a young Civilian who was "barbarously massacred by a mob of Mussalmen" at Cuddapah in 1832, and of Agnes, his wife, who died of a broken heart three weeks later at the age of twenty. Another slab in the same edifice commemorates a missionary whose "most meek demeanour" is eulogized. Pleasing as is the quality ascribed to the deceased, one may doubt whether he himself would have selected it for special mention in his epitaph. Old Town also possesses some mercantile buildings of the early days of the Company, to which body even now the ignorant occasionally allude as still in being and control.

No reference to Cuddalore would be complete without an allusion to that astonishing person Raworth, whose history is recorded in Mr. Francis' excellent *Gazetteer of South Arcot*. More than two centuries ago Raworth held a position which may be described as that of a Collector. For some reason or other he was placed under suspension, and one Davenport was ordered to relieve him. Raworth, however, had other views. He had created a party devoted to himself among the military whose "intolerably sottish and disorderly" conduct was a source of anxiety to the authorities at Fort St. George, and it was far from his intention to allow himself to be divested of office at Cuddalore. Therefore, when the new Collector arrived, he found himself resisted by force and had to retire. Returning with sixty "chosen men," he was fired on with cannon. There is a Canarese folk-song which describes an attack by our forces upon a fort in North Canara and declares that, "when the bullets fell among the English, they retired and wrote a report." So it was with Davenport. He retreated and reported the circumstances to the Government at Fort St. George. That body dealt with the crisis with energy and resolution. Having first recorded an opinion that it was necessary to "draw up a protest against Mr. Raworth for his unwarrantable way of proceeding," they took still more drastic measures. They sent two peacemakers, one being a chaplain, to remonstrate with Raworth about his "rash way of proceeding." That gentleman meanwhile had not been idle. He had spent the interval in vigorously attacking Davenport, with the result that several were killed and wounded on each side. Then the peacemakers arrived, but Raworth disdained to argue with them. All he would say was that, if the Governor came in person from Madras to parley with him, he would be prepared to resign his office on terms. The unfortunate Governor was so terrorized by his unruly subordinate that he actually came toiling by slow stages to Cuddalore. Then arrived the climax, for, as soon as that dignitary and his retinue came within the field of Raworth's activities, they found themselves, in the old chronicler's happily humorous phrase, "briskly entertained from the batteries with all the guns they could bring to bear." After this closing set-piece, Raworth, who on calm reflection felt that he had gone rather far, fled to Pondicherry, and thence he sailed for France, where oblivion unhappily falls on this bold and adventurous character. The Governor, who had done nothing, received, after the way of the world, a sword of honour in recognition of his services.

Attracted by its military and industrial associations, I went on to Porto Novo, but found there nothing worth seeing. The place shows, however, signs of unusual prosperity, and is better built than the ordinary village, which is still, in the main, composed of mean huts. It possesses an old Dutch cemetery which is "protected," and kept structurally in good order but was then being used by certain persons as a latrine, a fact which gave occasion to the Muhammadan gentleman accompanying me on my walk to inveigh against Hindu lack of reverence for the resting-places of the dead. It possesses, in addition, a river of some size, the banks of which bear an abundant growth of "tillai" trees. This tree is a sort of *excæcaria*, and it is said that anyone who falls asleep near one will awake with a swollen head. The symptomatic evidence seems to point to a wide geographical range on the part of this plant.

The finest rock-fort of Southern India, Gingee, is in this district, but I have not seen it. I did, however, make a pilgrimage to the thrice-holy temple of Chidambaram, and stood in the presence of the "Chidambara rahasyam," the Secret of Chidambaram, the invisible Etheric Lingam. As used in this connection, the last word has a special meaning, but, in a general sense, the lingam is the phallus, and in Southern India there are countless representations of it in stone; an object of reverence to the Saivite and of embarrassing questions on the part of travelling ladies. Externally the pagoda is of ordinary type, but, when the Nāttukkottai Chettis have composed their differences with the great administrative brotherhood of Dīkshitars, and have resumed their decorative labours which at that time had already accounted for some thirty lakhs of rupees, the interior is likely to be worthy of the renown of the fane. The place, as it then stood, left on the mind a confused impression of a jungle of carved pillars and of enormous toil undirected by art. The spacious enclosure contains several subsidiary shrines of which one is dedicated to Sakti, the Female Principle. There are also within it a fine, deep-sunken tank and a mantapam of great size, modern (as shown by the undravidian, high, vaulted roof which gives it somewhat the appearance of a Cathedral nave), and adorned with tawdry chandeliers and crude painting. To the temple proper the multitude of pillars gives, by reason of their size and monstrosity of design, a certain impressiveness which is augmented by the occasional, solemn clang of a bell. The existence of shrines of both Vishnu and Siva is an unusual feature of the place. Many Tamil hymns, fine hymns too, have celebrated the connection of the latter deity with this his favoured abode.

Section 10

TANJORE

The Tanjore temple has been mentioned already, but a few additional remarks about it may not be amiss. Apparently the main structure is assigned to the eleventh century, and, if this is so, it is quite one of the oldest temples now in use in Southern India. The plan is not the usual square with gopurams on each side, but an oblong with two gopurams only, and those on the same side. A paved way leads under these into a brick-floored courtyard, which has an air of spaciousness and unusual cleanliness. In the middle soars the high and shapely vimāna in the form of an oblong, truncated pyramid. The effect is good, although the ornamentation of the vimāna is on somewhat mean lines. Alongside the main structure stands the Subramanya shrine, the lower part of which is well carved, but it is not otherwise remarkable, and the praise lavished in books on this little building is perhaps excessive. On the wall of the cloister surrounding the courtyard are painted scenes from the incredibly grotesque Hindu mythology. The temple is the main show of Tanjore, but the Rajas' Palace must not be ignored. Of the history of the Marātha Kings of Tanjore, of their rise to power, vicissitudes and final loss of authority, it is unnecessary to say anything. Remains their abode, a maze of dirty, darksome passages and a huddled heap of worthless buildings. The last member of the dynasty, although already heavily married, distinguished himself by taking to his couch seventeen maidens in one year and survived the experience but a short time. There were other members of the family whose acquisitive tastes took different forms, and, as a consequence, there are to be found in the Palace a fine armoury containing some artistic weapons and a famous hoard of Oriental manuscripts, some of which are illuminated. The librarian who has charge of the manuscripts keeps also, under lock and key, an Indian *Ars libidinis*. I had not the courage to ask to see it, and decorum forbids me to repeat the remark about it which a Frenchman uttered in his surprise, but I understand that it is realistically, if crudely, illustrated.

There used to live at Tanjore a Roman Catholic poet of whose religious lays I possess some specimens in print. They are worthy of quotation *in extenso*, but, to economize space, I shall content myself with giving extracts from two of them. The first is from a hymn to St. Joseph:

> " Saint Joseph was the father-nurse
> Of our Lord Jesus Christ of Naz.
> Selected was he of mankind
> As purest rare of man to find.

> "Next to the stainless Virgin Mary
> Was he in virtue and chaste glory,
> Desired by the Holy Trinity
> To nurse the urchin Divinity.
>
> "As when below unanimous
> So now too as next of his Spouse
> Is vying as much to save souls,
> Confounding most the hellish moles."

Obscure, but so is Blake.

The next is from an address to "The mighty Rosary":

> "He who begins you once
> Your efforts much him charm
> Become disparted chums
> And grow more and more warm.
>
> "You are the telephone
> As well the telegraph,
> To carry our soul's tone
> To Mary, God and Staff."

"And staff" is particularly good, and the touch of modernity in the second verse will be admired. "Disparted chums" is, I take it, a synonym for "Inseparable friends."

The Collector of Tanjore lives some seven miles from the chief town, at a hamlet called Vallam. The way thither passes Kissing Corner, which recalls an old scandal in which a doctor and a young married lady were the principal *dramatis personæ*. The Collector's house, which consists of three blocks connected by long corridors, lies in a wooded hollow scooped out of a stretch of bare laterite. In the banyan opposite the entrance there remained for some years after his death traces of the arboreal porch which the long-limbed Saddler used as a substitute for an office-room. He was a vigorous shikāṛi in his youth, and supplied me with an excellent illustration of the uncertainty of sport even in so favourable a tract as Jeypore. He used to employ beaters by the hundred, and yet sometimes, for months together, could not get a shot. Then, once in a way, there would occur such a day as the one now to be described. He began it by wounding a bear. In following this, he put up a buffalo, which he wounded and turned off to follow. On the way another buffalo was sighted. This, too, he wounded and pursued. Whilst on the tracks of the second buffalo, he stumbled on and killed a bison. Afterwards the bear and one of the buffaloes were found dead.

Hatfield's brother R., a man of great prowess with the rifle, had a somewhat similar glut of business in the course of a day and a half. It began by his disturbing a tigress with a cub. She charged him at once and he dropped her dead. Later on he saw and wounded a bear, which also attacked and was killed at close quarters. The last encounter was with a wounded bison, and, when that laid its head down to charge, it flashed across R.'s mind that some Power not to be denied had resolved upon his death. Nevertheless he struck down his third antagonist also. On quite another occasion R. was attacked by a panther which he had wounded. His rifle jammed after the first shot, the animal sprang, R. ducked and, passing over him, it died as it alighted. I remember meeting a General B. who claimed to have destroyed forty tigers, seventy or eighty panthers, and some thirty bears. This is a colossal life's work, and apparently he was only once in trouble when a panther seized him by the arm, knocking him down, tore out a mouthful of flesh, then bit him through the thigh, and finally started to mangle his calf. A Sikh gallantly beat the animal off with a clubbed rifle, and B. was carried thirty miles to a railway station. On the way he got hold of some carbolic acid, which he applied undiluted to the wounds; an heroic course which proved too much for the germs.

Alongside the house at Vallam is a small ruined fort—when and by whom built I have forgotten—and in it is a magnificent well. The jungle growth in fort and garden affords a retreat for the birds to which the bare surroundings give no shelter, so that, at seasons, the place is as an aviary in the daytime, vibrant with trilling, whistling, and twittering, while at night the deep "Hoo" of the Great-eared owl tolls through the darkness.

To the new-comer in India the dominant note in the bird-orchestra is the caw of the crow, but older residents may incline to give pride of place to the tailor-bird. Once its sharp and varied cry, "to-whee, to-whee, to-whee," or "which-oo, which-oo, which-oo," is learnt, it is heard on all sides. One of our most beautiful birds is the honeysucker, or sunbird, in its various sorts. It is often spoken of as a humming-bird with more excuse than could have been pleaded by the Governor whom I heard pronounce, with the urbane finality appropriate to his office, the red-deer to be a rodent. I lifted a honeysucker's nest which was hanging loosely in a climbing plant to examine it, and, when the doorway of the domed house came in view as I turned it, behold, sticking out of it, the minute head and curved beak of the mother-bird unmoved by this convulsion of nature.

Every one knows the nest of the weaver-bird, that artfully twisted flagon with two necks. It is generally supposed to represent, in conjunction with its position, the last thing in life-saving apparatus, but it is not absolutely secure. Stark came to the edge of a tank wherein stood a tree laden with these nests, and, as he approached, some snakes which were swimming towards the tree turned back, but one had already got home. The tail was lashed round the upper neck of the nest, and the head was darting about the lower part, peeping and prying. At length the snake spied the opening of the lower neck, and by degrees it entered thereby, the tail cautiously shifting its hold lower and lower until the reptile was wholly inside, when there occurred movements which showed that a meal was in progress. Hatfield watched some weaver-birds building. From time to time all of them would fly away for material, all save one, a hen imbued with a clear conception of labour-saving devices. As soon as the others had departed, she started pulling fibres out of their nests and weaving them into her own. While they were present, her conduct was, of course, a model of propriety. Just a word or two more about birds.

There was a black-and-white robin which for five days haunted my house at Ootacamund. Hour after hour during that period it remained outside beating itself against the window-panes. If a window were opened, it flew off to a shut one and resumed its incomprehensible battle.

My butler owned a myna, one of the common southern sort. He used to let the bird out of its cage in order that it might, in his phrase, "graze about." During these outings the bird was said to fly often to a house at least half a mile away, where the butler's wife lived ; after spending some time with her, it would return to the cage.

Once, when I was sitting at work between two open windows, there was a rush and a scuffle, and I saw on my table a rainbow-hued bird. It sat there motionless within hand's reach until the rustling of a paper drove it in mad flight through the window.

It was that ground-thrush which they call in Hindustāni "nauranga," or "nine colours," and for which an appropriate name would be Rainbow bird. It has a singular taste for flying into houses, always headlong, and sometimes so recklessly as to kill itself against a wall. It is fairly common, but is rarely seen.

In Scotland where, as my Scotch friends assure me, Nature has lavished her choicest gifts upon man and beast, I chanced on a pretty example of the courage evoked by parenthood in the case of a couple of grouse. My companion picked up one of a brood of grouselings, and it cheeped. Instantly both the parents, which were flying off, wheeled back. The cock dashed towards us as if to attack, but, when a few yards distant, lost heart and turned tail. The hen settled close by and came creeping towards us, flattening herself against the ground and drooping her wings. When a yard from my companion she stopped and fixed her gaze upon him, and so stayed until he released the chick, when it and the mother-bird went off in different directions.

In the early part of my service I spent some weeks at Kumbhakōnam, a town in this district much affected by Brahmans. On arrival at the public bungalow I found there one F., a fiery-haired Engineer, hot from a conflict for which his opponents were not, perhaps, wholly blameworthy. F., going out for an evening stroll, met two natives who seemed disposed to walk him down, so he put his stick in front of him to clear, as it were, a way for himself. Doubtless this gave offence, for, as F. passed, one of the men hit him over the head with a bamboo and was knocked down in return. Then F. went back and brooded over the White Man's Burden until it became clear to him that he had been unwisely lenient. Accordingly he issued next day a notice that he was anxious to have an interview with the man assaulted by him on the previous day. Scenting compensation, some one, possibly a stranger innocent of any part in the fray, appeared at the bungalow and was asked to step inside. F. then shut the door upon him and set to work furiously with a horsewhip. "Run," he gasped at length, flinging open the door, but, even as the visitor complied, the heart of F. hardened within him; he felt the need for some finishing touches. The fugitive ran well, and F. had been able to get in only two or three more cuts before the snapping of his braces ended the chase.

Some years before that time there took place at Kumbhakōnam, as I was informed, a singular occurrence. There came to the town a man of religion who gave out that he had a special mission to women desirous of offspring. The remedy for sterility which he applied was the natural one, and his ministrations were effected, in such semi-privacy as a screen afforded, by the side of the temple tank. So entirely was the matter regarded as a religious rite that women resorted openly to the Saint. Report of what was taking place having reached the Government, they instructed the Superintendent of Police to interfere in the interests of morality, and the man was shifted.

As to the following anecdote, I can only say that I hope that it is not true. It relates to a distant time and, I think, to the district of Tanjore. C. was the District Judge, and, in accordance with the then practice, had the jail under his general charge. He told the jailor that he intended to go for a week to Yercaud, starting on the following Friday. The jailor reminded him that a prisoner was due to be hanged on the Wednesday after the day fixed for departure and, under the rules at that time in force, the Judge had to be present at the execution. C. thereupon had an interview with the condemned man, explained the circumstances, and begged that, as a personal favour, he would consent to be hanged on Friday instead of five days later. To this the convict, who must have been an uncommonly good fellow, agreed. Hanged he was accordingly and the Judge went off on his holiday. When he returned, the jailor, in an agony of fear, informed him that, on the day after his departure, a reprieve had arrived. C. thereupon instructed his subordinate to report that the man had died of cholera before effect could be given to the reprieve, and thus, with proper manipulation of the registers, the shameful transaction was concealed from the superior authorities.

SECTION II

ABROAD

A brief account of a few excursions to places outside the Presidency may now be given.

Of these the first was to Bījāpur in Bombay, a place of renown in days of yore. An outer circle of time-worn wall takes in a large area of flat and doleful country, in the middle of which the present-day inhabitants dwell in squalid fashion amidst the dust, dirt, and decay of ancient buildings and broken masonry. It is here that the Ādil Shāhi dynasty had its capital in the sixteenth and seventeenth centuries.

The best general view of the place is got from the Sāt Manjli, whence one sees "the hundred-gated circuit of the wall," the imposing defence works of the citadel, and a multitude of domes and shattered buildings. The material used in construction is a peculiarly lugubrious lava-stone, and it may be surmised that the removal from the ruins of all traces of vegetation has not been in every respect an advantage. Architects revel here in combinations of vaulting surfaces, corner squinches, and so on, but the ordinary man, too, finds a feast spread out. For me to suggest a choice among the many goodly structures on view would be an impertinence, but every one will take pleasure in one distinguishing feature of the Bījāpur mosques, namely, the ornamented stone frontlet which most of them bear round their brows. The learned would probably call this adornment a fascia. I cannot clearly describe it, but it is singularly beautiful. The landscape is dominated by the mighty Gōl Gumbāz, which is the tomb of Muhammad Ādil Shāh and is said to possess the largest dome in the world. It has a fine fascia ; otherwise it is very bare both inside and outside, and the ugliness of the inner plaster shell is redeemed only by its majestic proportions. On the floor are cenotaphs ; the real tombs stand veiled in darkness in a vault. Truly a noble oblation to Death.

Some little distance from the modern town is a place called Naurāzpur, where stand together the graves of some sixty women. The tombs are identical in shape and age, and legend may be justified in asserting that they contain the bones of the wives of a super-Bluebeard, Afsab Khān, who drowned them when he felt his own end approaching. The pond close by may have played a part in the ghastly drama

I have spoken before of that quality of grace and cleanliness which is a distinguishing feature of mosque architecture, and becomes a place of prayer so much better than the gloom and oily dirtiness of the Hindu temple. This character is somewhat wanting at Bījāpur owing to the dinginess of the stone used in construction, but no one will regret having gone out of his way to see the very remarkable group of Muhammadan buildings which this town contains.

My next foreign journey took me to Mysore, where I was entertained as a State guest in the building which is now called Government House, and which is said to have been constructed for Sir John Malcolm a century or so ago. It is a fine house, palatially furnished, and I was treated there much to my satisfaction.

Mysore has two objects of interest: a small zoological garden with which must be coupled the Maharaja's flock of llamas, and the new palace of that ruler which is, perhaps, the most painfully inartistic building in the world. In that edifice stained-glass windows and macaw-hued cast-iron columns are engaged in a polychromatic struggle of so frightful a character, that the eye turns almost with relief towards the heavily massed gilding. That, however, is as the sun in his midday power, and at this stage an examination of the glossy pictures on the walls is useful to secure gradation in the return to normal vision. When that has been reached, the visitor will be in a position to consider the relative degrees of hideousness of silver, ivory, and ivory-inlaid rosewood as material for doors. The building does, however, contain some good carving in stone and wood, and handsome decorative stone has been employed in the construction of it. Also strange weapons are to be seen in the adjacent armoury.

I drove out some miles to have a look at Seringapatam, the old fortress so attractively situated by a rushing, rocky river. History peoples the fort with miserable English prisoners and fills it with the clamour of avenging stormers, but nothing in the place attracted my notice so much as the Daryā Daulat, the fanciful little pavilion of Tippu Sahib. I spent some quiet hours there, looking out on a sunny, well-kept garden. The building is of two floors with rooms communicating by multifoil arches, and every bit of the inside is covered with gilding, silvering, or paint so mellowed that the profusion of tints gives only an air of appropriate gaiety. The outside of this summer-house is of no account, and the quaint alfresco picture of Colonel Bailly's defeat at Perumbākkam is not in keeping with the character of the building. Not far off are the tombs of Hyder Ali and Tippu. To these the surrounding trees and a cypress avenue give import. The tombs have some handsome pillars of a polished black stone, the peculiar graining of which lends to the smooth surface an appearance of unevenness. The sandalwood-and-ivory doors, which are said to have been added in the time of Lord Dalhousie, give fragrance to the air but offend by their incongruity.

It is but a short distance from the fort to the well-known Deserted House. The story goes that a certain Colonel Scott, already stricken by the death of his wife, returned from parade one morning to find his two daughters lying dead of cholera and, distraught with grief, flung himself into the river alongside. A more prosaic version is that he simply fled from the ill-omened spot. Anyway there was in what happened a distressfulness so sharp as to move the Maharaja to order that the house should be left for ever as it stood on that tragic day. As a fact there is now hardly any furniture left; only a couple of queer, high bedsteads, a curious sideboard, a table, two or three chairs, and a carpet. There are also some pictures of incredible badness. The house is merely an ugly, dirty tenement which in nowise repays a deviation to inspect, but those who take pleasure in vulgarity and silliness will find plenty to their taste in the remarks written by various hands in the Visitors' Books kept on the premises.

Mysore is often spoken of as "the model State," and is, at all events, a Paradise for the indigenous Brahmans, of whom I have come across some particularly well-looking and well-mannered specimens. Conditions are not, I have heard, quite so delightful for the non-Brahmans. Official arrangements used to be so admirably designed as to supply in the Secretariat one clerk for every three papers available for disposal daily. It may be different now.

The main object of the journey to Ceylon was to see the ancient Buddhist town of Anurādhapura, more commonly called Anurājapura. My wife and I reached that place in the dead hours of a rainy night, and were conveyed in bullock-coaches from the railway station to an apparently deserted building in the depths of a forest. After some delay a lamp was lit and we were admitted to wringing-wet beds in a room of neglected appearence. Under the light of day the hotel wore a less disconsolate aspect, and we found ourselves in a well-wooded country over which we wandered for a couple of days with a diminutive guide of the Singhalese race. Huge, bulbous growths push upwards through the foliage, monstrous, solid hemispheres of brick covering, one presumes, relics of the Blessed One. They are called dāgobas, or, to translate, Tooth-shrines, and are, for the most part, shrub-grown, half ruinous, and bereft of their "tees," or apical umbrella-ornaments. The highest, as it stands, attains some 260 feet. Of interest, save as monuments of old-time toil in the cause of religion, they possess none, being things appreciable as well in a photograph as *in situ*.

But the Usurumuniya pagoda, built on and around

a mass of dark rock, is quite charming in its general effect in spite of the hideousness of the large, new hall wherein a gramophone has been installed, to mingle, one presumes, its metallic and vulgar outpourings with the prayers of the worshippers. It was at this place that an officious and ill-mannered youth, unconnected with the pagoda, took objection to our entering part of the building in boots. The priest entertained no such objection, and the youth's action was symptomatic, not of religious sentiment, but of the growth of hostility towards Europeans.

A handsome bit of stone-carving in semicircular form, known as a Moonstone, is dwelt upon ecstatically in the guide-books, but is repeated *ad nauseam*, and there seems to be no other sculpture worth seeing except a graceful figure of a Serpent-spirit. The famous Bō tree, whatever its true history, is to the eye of the non-Buddhist only an ordinary specimen of *Ficus religiosa*, and, on the whole, Anurādhapura is a somewhat disappointing place.

A drive of eight miles, in the course of which one may chance on elephants, through jungle of medium height, brings one to Mihintala. The hill looks over the great interior forest of Ceylon. It is a sacred spot and the peacefulness which enwraps it makes it seem so, albeit the dāgoba is an ugly thing, and the new structures alongside are out of keeping with their surroundings. Building was still in progress, and, on our way down, we met bands of pilgrims in clean white cloths, each carrying a brick to aid in the work, and at intervals cheering and chanting hymns in that high, unpleasant, nasal key which, in India too, constitutes singing.

Kandy was our next destination, and it is reached through as lovely a bit of tropical scenery as one can want to see. Notwithstanding an elevation of 1600 feet, Kandy is enervating to a marked degree, but it is a pretty place with a sheet of water and low wooded hills. The famous Peradeniya Botanical Gardens are close by. Unfortunately I missed Mr. Lock, the then Superintendent of the Gardens, so well known as the author of "Variation, Heredity, and Evolution." In addition, Kandy possesses a Museum which would, I am sure, be interesting if it contained any exhibits. There used to be Kings of Kandy, and their gold-plated throne, a tolerable piece of work, is used on occasion by His Majesty at Windsor. Their descendants seem to be legion. As Collector, I was always having correspondence about youths who were in receipt of allowances as members of the Kandyan family.

From this place the railway ascends to Nuwara Eliya (pronounced New-railya). The intervening country must have been beautiful once, but the planting industry has reduced it to dull commonplaceness until the altitude is reached at which the Government have imposed a check upon the merciless skinning of the hills. As an example of industrial brutality towards Nature, this part of the mountains of Ceylon may be forcibly cited. Nuwara Eliya, being 6,200 feet above the sea, is comfortably cool and it is an attractive enough little place. We drove to Hakgalla, a short distance away, to see the Botanical Gardens, but mist hid from us the much-praised view of the lower hill-country which is to be got thence. This passing glimpse of Ceylon left on my mind the impression that the buildings of the country are of no intrinsic merit. The old work probably owed any effect it had to mere size, while the new is conspicuously trivial and even vulgar.

SECTION 12

THE WEST COAST

On revient toujours à ses premiers amours, and in later years my feet strayed at times into the Eden wherein part of my youth was spent. Generally my destination was East Hill, near Calicut, whence the Collector of Malabar overlooks a sea of coco-nut fronds. It is an agreeable home, with a superb glazed verandah and a timber-built dining-room open to the wandering breeze and suggestive in some delightful way of the cabin of an old wooden ship. At night an armed guard stands at the entrance. No other Collector receives this protection, which originated with the murder of Mr. Conoly, who, some sixty or seventy years ago, was hacked to death in the presence of his wife in the verandah by Moplahs armed with the big war-knives which they used to carry.

There seems to be something about the West Coast people and especially about the great landholders of Malabar which renders them less remote from Englishmen than the East Coast folk, and I have found Collectors of Malabar to be always enthusiastic over their noble domain, and generally anxious to save its interesting and peculiar customs from the ever-threatening waves of Tamilism and Occidentalism. I remember one of these Nāyar landholders very well, partly because he was of a rare type, an Indian of a jocular cast, partly because he died in my presence just after delivering a speech, and partly because of an account which he gave me of a peculiar form of sport practised in Malabar. A party goes into the jungle at night, one member bearing on his head, in a sort of metal poke-bonnet, flaming material which throws a strong light ahead. In the obscurity at each side walks a man with a gun. The fire-bearer dances along, jingling bells on a stick. Animals of all sorts, even occasionally tigers and, more strangely still, snakes, fascinated by the light and the noise, will, it is said, approach within a yard or so of the beacon and so expose themselves to destruction. It is, however, the practice, when a dangerous animal appears, to quench the light, whereupon the beast makes off. My informant asserted that Spotted-deer have been known to come right up to the man carrying the light and to place their forefeet on his shoulders, in which event they are supposed to have taken him for Siva and to be in process of worshipping him. Lascelles spent an eerie night in the jungle trying this form of sport, but the only thing he came on was a cow which he had himself tied up as a bait for a tiger.

A man named Mead whom I once met, had a lively experience with a rogue elephant in Malabar. When he first saw the animal, it was standing with the head hidden by a tree, but he essayed a shoulder shot and the beast disappeared in the grass. He thought that it was down, but the grass was higher than he fancied. In fact the elephant was afoot and its trunk was waving about over the grass like a leech seeking for his wind. This found, the animal charged. Mead was standing up against an impenetrable barrier of thorns a little above the elephant, between which and himself was a low bank rendered slippery by the rain which was beating down pitilessly. The check which this bank caused was probably the saving of the man. As the rogue came on, Mead met it with a ball in the head which knocked it down. Rising it charged again, only to meet a like fate. A third time the rush was made, and a third time the courageous animal fell. Mead was by now so wearied by the strain and by the ceaseless, blinding downpour that he resolved to end the matter one way or another, so he moved down the slope towards the elephant. Fortunately it was unable to get up for a fourth attack, and another bullet despatched it.

On one of my voyages I got to know a man who was employed by the Burma Trading Company, and who some five years before had had charge of some elephants. One of these turned savage and started killing or trying to kill people, for which reason Smith mounted an elephant and hastened to the scene. The must elephant charged Smith's elephant as soon as it came in view, and ripped up the pad with a tusk. The pad-elephant thereupon bolted, with its assailant in pursuit. Smith and the mahout were swept off by a branch. The latter climbed a tree, but the former was half stunned and recovered his senses just in time to catch a whiff of the must elephant's foul breath as he was whirled past it in the grip of the trunk. The elephant brought him down with a bang on the ground and, kneeling, tried to gore him. Failing in this, the brute swung him up again, brought him down once more, and was repeating its attempt to gore him when another man came up on an elephant of which the bully stood in awe, and before which it took to flight. Smith had his hip grazed by a tusk, all the skin taken off his back, the jaw smashed in two places and two ribs broken, and sustained such a shock that his nerves were even then not fully under control.

A propos of elephants, I was informed by a man whose word on matters of woodcraft was not to be disputed, that these animals are in the habit of swallowing whole the fruit known as the wood-apple, which is about the size of an orange and has a hard, woody shell. The fruits are passed out in the same condition, that is, unbroken, the rinds showing neither crack nor hole, and yet, in some way or other, the pulpy contents are absorbed during the passage. These empty shells are collected and used as snuff-boxes.

One of my hosts at East Hill was Owen, a man so intolerant of official criticism that, when Inspecting Officers, intent on business, came to stay with him, he would deliberately frustrate the object of their visits by exposing in a prominent position a magnificent French edition of the Arabian Nights, unexpurgated. I made with Owen the tour which I am about to describe. He had a quiet, somewhat languid, manner, but during that tour, after I had been his companion for a fortnight, upon the most trifling provocation, he turned with fist and foot upon a cooly in a frenzy of exasperation which I have never been able to account for.

We went from Trichūr to the small bungalow on the coast at Chetwāyi, travelling five miles across a lagoon in a curious way, for our boat moved along a strip of water considerably above the surface of the lake. It was in this wise. Two rows of poles are run across the lagoon and bamboo mats are fixed between the poles. Then the people start to bale the lagoon dry enough for rice-growing by lifting the water into the trough formed by the mats, so that in time there results a sort of aqueduct which serves as a highway for boats. The lifting of the water is done for the most part by means of large wheels with blades attached and projecting spokes. A man keeps the wheel revolving and the blades lifting the water by stepping from one projecting spoke to another, much as a treadmill is worked. A more usual mode of raising water in the south is by the picottah, which consists of an upright post on which swings a long pole with a leather bag or iron bucket at one end. The other end is fitted with pegs, and by the movement of a man up and down these pegs the bag is lifted full and lowered empty. During this process the worker chants in a monotonous and rather agreeable way. I saw a poem called "The song of the picottah," which contains the sort of things which the worker ought to say on such occasions, but I believe that he merely sings out the number of bagfuls discharged.

Chetwāyi is on a wide and deep backwater which extends worthwards to Calicut and southwards for a much greater distance. It swarms at this point with crocodiles, some of great size. I went out in a canoe after them with a man who turned up unexpectedly at the bungalow, but we did not hit any. On our way back I was regaled by my companion with a sketch of the life of a person I knew by name. This individual, it seems, began life as a sailor and then joined the Salt Department, which he left under suspicion of having extracted ten thousand rupees from the treasury in his charge. So qualified, he started a bank and figured as a leader of society until he was found to be embezzling the funds entrusted to him, and received a sentence of imprisonment for eighteen months. He had incurred liabilities during his period of social success, and the creditors arranged to have him arrested for debt on his release from jail, but he had taken the precaution to enter prison with sovereigns concealed in the soles of his boots, and with these he had bought a uniform from one of the warders. Thus disguised, he slipped past his victims and escaped into French territory.

Owen and I left Chetwāyi in valloms, which are large canoes with a tilt of "tatty," or platted palm-leaves, and found ourselves by morning in a narrow freshwater reach covered with the blossoms of lotuses and the beautiful, noxious water-hyacinth.

A hovel on the bank gave us shelter until the next morning, when "twelve rowers, with the impulse of thought" and to the strains of a weird melody, paddled us six miles to meet a smart motor-launch, in which we did the remaining twenty-one miles to Cochin.

I liked the quarters we found for ourselves at that place, for we were right up against the beach and saw the boats passing in and out through the sea-passage, and the "Chinese nets" swinging up and down all day on the water's edge.

Cochin has a bad reputation for disease, especially for that disgusting complaint elephantiasis, which is sometimes called Cochin leg, and the town, which is cooped up between sea and backwater, is crowded and noisome. Nevertheless it possesses things of interest. A Portuguese church, now used by the Anglicans, is perhaps the oldest European place of worship in India. The interior is plain but on good, spacious lines, and round the walls are memorial slabs rich with armorial bearings and dating back to 1524. Vasco da Gama was buried here, but his body was removed later to Portugal. There are also communities of White and Black Jews, the former betraying outlandish origin by their pallid, rather than fair, skins; the latter to appearance autochthonous. The White Jew synagogue is the more interesting. It possesses huge rolls of parchment containing the Law in Hebrew, some remarkable silver ornaments, and a large crown with pendants. About these parts dwell also the Syrian Christians, who claim an antiquity in Christianity reaching back to the first century, but nothing certain is known about the origin of either them or the Cochin Jews. My experience of the Syrian Christians as officials has led me to form a high opinion of their qualities.

On our departure from this place, we ran in the launch down the unending backwater, the sea close alongside, for ninety miles, until the banks rose into miniature, wooded cliffs between which the waterway wound and widened in reach and mere. On the shore of the backwater, just before Quilon is gained, stands a fine, spacious house which used to be a perquisite of the office of Resident in Travancore. It is furnished in lordly fashion, and we found too late, after we had settled down in the Club, that it had been prepared for our reception.

Close to Quilon is the little British *enclave* of Tangassēri, ninety-nine acres in extent. It consists of a bit of a shore bearing the inevitable coco-nut trees, a lighthouse, fragments of a Portuguese fort, and a group of small, whitewashed houses ; really nothing at all and yet, I can hardly say why, I found it charming.

Still twenty-eight miles on and the southernmost piece of British territory on the West Coast was reached. It is styled Anjengo, and is composed of 279 acres of sand and palms carved out of the Travancore State. Its existence is due to the small fort on the shore where the English were allowed to establish themselves in 1695, and outside of which is the grave of a young Englishwoman who died in 1704. It is somewhat strange that this minute speck of the Empire should have been the birthplace of two persons whose names are familiar to thousands: Robert Orme, the historian, and Eliza Draper, the friend of Sterne.

If the two or three ports be left out of consideration, there are few places more melancholy than the stretch of coast to which the backwater we followed gives noiseless access. On the one side the coco-nut palms droop listlessly in serried, unbroken array, mile after mile, mile after mile. On the other side palms again or mournful flats, dumb and featureless. There is nothing on which Time can set his mark. Always it was thus, and always it will be thus. Only, here and there, a small house among the trees tells of the shadow which is Man.

EPILOGUE

TRADITION tells of a certain youthful philosopher who divided human life into three stages by definitions in the following terms : " When a man is young, he thinks of all the wicked things he will do when he grows up. This is called the Age of Innocence. When he grows up, he does the wicked things he thought of as a boy. This is called the Prime of Life. When he is old, he repents of the wicked things he has done. This is called Dotage or Senile Decay."

There is strong temptation to employ this third period in writing reminiscences as well as in doing penance for past sins, and the impulse in the former direction has proved too strong for me, conscious as I am that such trivial wares as I have to offer are not likely to command much market.

Especially do I deplore my lack of that art of portraiture which might confer a measure of diuturnity upon some of the good fellows who made their Indian pilgrimage along with me. One would fain postpone for them the contumelious day when

" No one will ask
Who or what they have been,
More than he asks what wave,
In the moonlit solitude mild
Of the midmost ocean, has swelled,
Foamed for a moment and gone."

INDEX